BEDAZZLED

"I Know How To Make People Go My Way, Uhh Almost.."

SAUMYA ARYA

BookLeaf Publishing
India | USA | UK

Presentation by *BookLeaf Publishing*

Web: www.bookleafpub.com
E-mail: info@bookleafpub.com

ISBN: 9789369538904

First edition 2025

To Vandana Gupta,

My mother, my friend, my life.

ONE

Mum didn't tell me that our landlord was the type of guy that makes girls swoon and fuss over him.

Oh shi-kerdookies!! In that dark blond hair, he looked like a model.

What Mum did tell me was that we were going to rent a ranch-style home with a family. That they had a yummy son, was not at all announced.

As Mum spotted Mr Keberkil, her childhood bestie Andrea Keberkil's husband, she waved and ushered me towards them. Mr Keberkil was a tall, bearded man, in his early forties, with a mischievous smile and just a hint of a protruding belly. His wife, Mrs Keberkil, was the vision of a typical housewife, with her thin, debilitated blonde hair pulled back in a bandana and a nude lipstick as a sorry excuse for makeup.

Surely it wasn't my fault that my eyes glued themselves to the absolutely luminous guy standing beside them. He was wearing a white graphic tee with jeans and had an alluring expression. Mum shook hands with Mr Keberkil while Mrs Keberkil, henceforth addressed as Andrea, embraced her in a bear hug. Andrea's eyes widened when she saw me but she quickly masked her reaction by saying, "Aaliah! Look at how pretty you've grown to be! And your hair! It's so long and uh... glamorous!" Well.

I know my pink woollen dress clashed horribly with my scarlet hair but the eight-hour flight demanded comfort and this is how far I could tone down my usual style. And his son, Mr Amazing-Height made me wish I had worn heels instead of my black-and-pink casual tennis shoes.

Andrea turned towards the man-tower, "And this is my son Baldasser, who not only excels in academics but also plays as the centre forward on his school football team! I am so proud of him!" The object of her praise just looked embarrassed.

But then he smiled and said, "Hey, call me Daze." Oh, fu-dge nuggets! His smile was adorable. He picked up our duffel bags as we exited the airport.

The weather outside was hazily cool. The atmosphere was pristine and clean. I followed Daze to their Nissan Terrano, and the guys sat in the front while the mothers chatted away, catching up. I felt a personal williwaw in my ears as I tried to tune out their conversation. When I looked up at the rearview mirror, I caught Daze's eye. He smiled at me with a look that seemed to say, "I know what you're feeling like." Mustering up my hottest smile, only displaying my upper set of teeth, I tried to create a lazy romantic effect. After that, we kept giving each other, what I imagined, flirty looks for the rest of the journey. Perchance, getting Daze to be my boyfriend was going to be effortless. I could imagine this neat dude with his arm around me treading across the town. I will obviously be popular with his friends, that has never been a hard job. We would go to dance clubs and lounges and... wait till everyone sees me getting dropped off to school by this piece of Captain Smooth.

Oh! This reminded me… "Mum, where am I going this semester?" Mr Keberkil answered instead, "You'll be going to the same school as Daze here—St. Regis Ruler College."

Mahvelous!! Spared from the feeling of being a lonesome stranger at the new school! I happily resumed my day dreaming. This guy deserved a girlfriend who was mercilessly sexy, a show-off and just a pinch of nasty. He deserved *me*. We were sooo going to be the power couple at St. Regis. Oh man, I could already see it all.

The street where the Keberkils lived had no fences separating the neighbours' gardens. The house was surrounded by shrubs of some kind and the garden was a carpet of purple pansies. I mean, the whole garden was purple! It appeared to be kind of hideously witchy, for someone as un-abnormal as Daze. Imagine paying rent for this (aka my reality). The only concrete I could see was the space in front of the garage which was front-facing. The house was single-storey, displaying beige-cream walls with maroon-tiled hip roof. I observed four large windows just at the front. Man... which of these were mine?

"The right side of the home is ours and the left is yours. We'll share the living room and the kitchen, of course," informed Andrea, giving a little too high-pitched giggle.

I was expecting more purples and pinks inside but a closer look revealed lemon-yellow walls, grey cotton sofas, chrome tables, bright miniature modern arts, intensely coloured silk cushions and an unimaginably tall bamboo plant at the corner. Man, Andrea cleaned up well.

I was so absorbed in the sudden change of scene that I didn't notice when Andrea took Mum to show her her room. I looked around the living space and found Daze smiling at me. Oh, fudge nuggets! I tried to say 'meow' with my eyes as I shrugged (Don't try this at home if you have eye-shoulder coordination issues).

"C'mon, I'll take you to your room."

"Will you really? That would be so helpful!" I responded in my best distressed-damsel-in-an-Avril-Lavigne-music-video voice.

My room had two windows side by side, blue walls, and a wooden floor. The room had a sunny look. I liked it.

"I'll help you move your furniture and stuff when the trucks reach here. Dad said they'll be here in two-three hours so..." he trailed off, looking at me expectantly with that same adorable smile.

"Yes, please, I would LOVE that!" I said in my most persuasive voice. It must have worked because he smiled at me for a few seconds and then checked me out while leaving the room.

It took me a while to decide where my furniture would go. The window at the right-hand side wall, where I would put my bed, gave a view of the hideous purple garden and the road. The one on the left looked out onto the street at the back.

Onwards to the bathroom: pristine with white walls and black floor tiles. The curtains didn't match the carpet or uh, what do they say when they wanna establish that it's not how it looked from the outside? The interiors were quite glam.

I went back to the room to figure out and plan the placement of my ample belongings which were on their way.

"Do you like it, Ally?" Mum came barging in, grinning.

"It's mah-velous, Mum!" I matched her smile, meaning it. Then I remembered something I had been meaning to ask her since we reached here. "Mum, how much do the Keberkils know about Dad?"

Mum looked away. "Andrea has always been a close friend of mine and therefore I have told her everything."

I had seen this coming. I let out an exasperated sigh which fluttered through my scarlet hair. "Mah-velous," I began sarcastically. "Now Daze will think I'm a freak."

Mum squinted at me. "What's so freaky about a girl whose father was shot helping the police for a noble cause? Was it his fault that he was using his special abilities to catch bad guys?" She paused and took a shaky breath. "You should be proud of your father, Aaliah. He was a true patriot."

"OF COURSE, I am proud of him, Mum, but that's not the point! You are totally misunderstanding... oh, forget it! What I meant was, I hope you haven't told them about *my* abilities."

She seemed incredulous. "Absolutely not, Ally! Your gift is a secret between us and will remain so."

I rolled my eyes. "Don't call it that."

Mum looked amused. "What? Your Gift?"

I glared at her. Some gift. Huh.

Have you ever looked at someone's eyes and felt instantly attracted? And I am not talking about mere infatuation here. What I am referring to is that moment when you are unable to break eye contact with the person and you start feeling stupefied; time appears to slow down and slumber lingers in the air. When you wake up from the trance, you cannot clearly recall what happened in the meantime. You are lucky if you haven't experienced this yet. This phenomenon is known as *hipnozes njerezore*. The ones who can practise this are known as Zaekhurus.

My father was a Zaekhuru. He worked in the CIA, naturally. The suspects used to be interrogated by him. While the other officers relied on threats and even assaults in the worst cases, my dad could get the person under investigation to confess his misdeeds in just five minutes. He'd get it taped in a voice recorder, with the suspect unharmed at that.

But this 'gift,' as Mum calls it, came with severe conseq—

What's that fudging honking? Oh, the movers' trucks are here. So, my stuff has finally arrived. Mah-velous! Time to call Daze.

The drawing room opened into the kitchen, which connected the Keberkils and Daze's rooms. There was a simple surfboard propped up by the door to Daze's room. On closer inspection, there was an eye drawn on it. Weird. But the guy could surf, right? I knocked. Got a grunt in reply. Hmm. Narrowing my eyes, I entered.

Blue. Everywhere. Different shades of blue on the walls, blue wardrobe, blue throw pillows, little blue circular carpets… and is that a blue giraffe SOFT TOY?

Shikerdoodles... here I was thinking *I* bled blue. I relished in the 'bluety' of the room... uh, deliberately avoiding the giraffe. He was sitting with his back towards me on this cupboard desk; Daze, I mean, not the giraffe; writing something, probably doing his homework.

I approached him checking out the neat cupboard. Some textbooks—Physics, Maths, Chemistry, Boring, a blue glass jar filled with some red pickle-y pasty stuff …what's that?

Daze gave me a once over and I noticed how small his ears were. "What's what?"

Shikerdoodles. Said that out loud, did I? Too late to back out now. I pointed towards the blue jar, "That…"

His gaze followed my finger. "That? That's Basil-flavoured Tomato sauce."

"But shouldn't that be in the kitchen?" Shut up. Don't judge him. Or at least don't make it *obvious* that he is being judged.

"Nah, that'd be too inconvenient at the rate I need to keep consuming it. Mum makes it at home specially for me. She says it keeps one's head stable and sturdy."

Need to keep consuming? Like a medicine? Tomato sauce at home? Okayyyy…?

"The trucks are here…" And he's true to his word when it comes to unloading, thanks to the… sauce?

The knock on my door interrupts the critical examination of my wardrobe. It is Daze, who first makes sure that I am alone, then proceeds to give me one of those slow smiles (Not creepy, just shy). I realised my cheeks must have been matching my pink dress in reaction.

"Hey, Daze… sup?"

Daze took in my room and his eyes rested on my bed. "Don't tell me you worship blue too! Cool uh..." He gestured in circular motions with his hands. "...sheets and stuff!"

I smiled my sexy tongue-behind-teeth smile (addressed as ToBT smile henceforth). "You can say that…"

After all, who doesn't like blue? Daze looked at me for a moment, his eyes smiling. "Aaliahhh," he pronounced my name with a sigh at the end. "I was wondering if you would do me the honour of being my pillion for school tomorrow?"

What in the fudge-nuggeting world is a pillion? Sounds like a flour-doll of a food fetishist.

"...Sorry? Your what?"

"My pillion." Daze looked shy all of a sudden. "I mean, would you let me give you a ride to school?"

I let that sink in. He must have misinterpreted my silence as bafflement.

"I mean, you know, I'll be going there anyway and I have no problem so, you know, if you want, or like, there's always a seat, and it's not necessary but like, I would—"

"Daze." In spite of my obvious ecstasy I somehow managed to keep a straight face. "That would be mah-velous."

Daze visibly relaxed. Man, this chunk of luxury chocolate was nervous asking *me* out! Um, well not literally *out* but you know what I mean. "So do you have a spare helmet that might fit me?"

Time to find out whether he has a girlfriend or not. Daze looked at me sheepishly and ran a hand through the back of his hair. Gosh, he was cute. I wondered how his hair would feel tangled in my fingers.

"...Nah, but if you feel the road is too bumpy, you can always trust and hold onto me."

Ooh, he was flirting. AND single. I nodded encouragingly, which brought my headache into focus. Suddenly, I was tired. "Alright then, I'll see you tomorrow morning, where you'll be my ride..."

Daze raised his eyebrows and too late, I realised how inappropriate that sounded. "Uhh..." I giggled and so did he.

"Gotcha," he turned and walked away. "I'll be your ride."

I settled into my bed, still in my hooded lounge dress and underwear. Sleeping will probably cure this ache I'd brewed up since entering the Keberkil household. Nightmares of bearded men and semi-naked tribals interacting plagued me almost throughout the night.

I was still sleepy when my alarm went off at 6 a.m. Shikerdoodles, the headache still lasted. I looked out the windows towards the purple garden. The lane was very quiet. Hmm... *I'm up too early*, I thought.

After the shower, I stood in front of my wardrobe. I had to blend in as much as possible. My scarlet hair won't let that happen but I still had to try. I decided to go with the Beige sweater dress and black tennis sneakers to match my black belt. A quick comb through my hair tamed it well enough. Just a bit of kohl, eyeliner and lip balm, and I was ready by 7.

The motorcycle ride as Daze's pillion to St. Regis Ruler was mostly pleasant, except for a certain pothole-ridden area. Was it my imagination or did Daze deliberately ride through them so that I'd lean more towards him? Anyway, I was more than happy to go along with it!

We passed by a florist's market and a few adorable cafes. St. Regis stood as a no-nonsense, blue and white building, about 4 stories high and stretching over the length of two football fields. I was still revelling in the sheer size of the school, when Daze drove through the main iron gates, and turned right to a low Brobdingnagian shed, which on further observation turned out to be a parking lot. As I climbed down and adjusted my wool dress, trying not to give everyone a glimpse of my skin-coloured boy shorts, something soft brushed past my back. "Daaaze! Hii!" chirped the brown-haired girl in the worn-out fleece dress. She had a rosebud mouth and abraded Vans.

Daze finished locking his helmet to his motorcycle. "Hey Caecilia, how's it going?" he inquires coolly.

"Gee, did you see how *breathtaking* Tyrion was in last night's episode! He totally convinced the hill tribes to be allies!" Caecilia gushes when she speaks, and though she is quite plain to look at, her manner is certainly endearing.

I look at Daze to see how he beholds her OBVIOUS adoration, but he's examining me instead—well, to be honest, my bosom.

Noticing his preoccupied interests, I smile at Caecilia, "Hey, I feel Bronn and Tyrion are the funniest characters. I'm Aaliah, cool school you've got here." The spell is broken as Caecilia takes a gander at me for the first time and her smile recedes.

"Ahem, yeah. Ally, she's Caecilia, my friend and classmate, and Caecilia, meet Ally, she lives with me now!" he grins.

What an eerie introduction. I can see how startled Caecilia is, her eyes wide. Whether it's because of my scarlet hair or something else, is a mystery. For two seconds, there's silence. "I've known Daze since we were 7 but I never heard him mention any Ally..." she mutters audibly.

OH, so that's how it's gonna be! She's declared territory! "Well, I *do* hope you have had better topics of conversation than 'The Ally diaries' in all these years..." I reply giggling sweetly.

Meanwhile, Daze walked out of the shed to clasp hand and do that shoulder-kiss thingy boys do as a fantastical excuse for a greeting, with a bulky guy in a crewcut. We stride towards them and I lay my eyes on the girl in a navy blue cashmere dress, whose waist was wrapped around in the Bulkyboy's arm as he gestured enthusiastically to Daze. Bulky appeared to be passionate about whatever they were discussing. Caecilia paces ahead and they all exchange salutations. A moment later, Daze turned his head and his hand found my shoulder. "Fadil, Edie, welcome Ally! She's my tenant and y'all's new classmate! Ally, this brute here is Fadil and he's the star athlete of our school, and this is Edie, his girlfriend and our budding artist. Hey Edie, don't you wanna do a portrait of Ally and her beautiful hair?" Daze jests.

Edie took in my appearance, her eyes crawling from my head and lingering a second too long at my legs. What. Was I getting goosebumps on my legs? Hate when that happens. Don't look, Ally. Don't loo—

"Hi...D'you like my sneakers, Edie?" I smiled flatly as I extended my hand towards her. Startled, she took my hand speechlessly and looked up at me even though I'm just 5'6". Fadil nodded at me and his huge trapezius muscle flexed.

We walked inside the building and down the corridor that had rooms on one side and an ample playground on the other.

Shikerdookies, there was more than one playground. There were basketball courts, a cricket field, football ground, cemented plains—the whole works.

Assemblages of young girls in floral shirt dresses stared at me—um, my hair—pausing in the middle of their conversations. Young boys mostly clad in plaid patterns hung about in groups by the cafeteria near the ground. The corridor ended at a crossway, opening to the grounds on one side and another set of rooms with the walls painted with the school logo (a globe wearing a crown) on the other.

"Ally, Vindu'zz offize is in here..." drawled Fadil. While I stared blankly, Edie translated in a soft voice, "He—ahem, he means our principal father Navindu's office is, eh, in there to the right. You'll be given your subject's table in there. Shall I show you?"

I looked at Daze, who was busy chatting with Caecilia, in all her wide eyes innocence.

"I'll catch up with you guys later according to my subject schedule, 'kay?" I said loudly.

Daze finally noticed. He came over, smiling. Man, his chest looked so broad in that grey T-shirt. "All the best, Ally. Hope you'll find me in most of your classes..."

YUM. I nodded back, looking up at him, and gave him a wink as I turned to go. He did want me in his classes, this must mean something!

The door to the office was ajar and there was no one behind the desk at the moment. The office had wood walls and flooring, giving it a warm feel. It looked pretty much like any principal's office except for a plate that said "Keep off the barb wire," which had inspired a graffiti underneath it. "But what did she do?" I smiled as I sat down on one of the vacant waiting chairs. A moment later, a tall blonde girl strolled in. She was wearing a dark lace slip dress with inserts that gave her a flattering cleavage. Man, that sexy dress must have turned a lot of heads. She sat down, and noticing my gaze, stared right back at me with a 'couldn't-care-less' half-lidded look. Her eyes, ridden with smudged muddy-toned eyeshadow, were beautiful. In fact, this girl was gorgeous.

"...What anime character are *you* supposed to be?" she asked in a drugged voice that matched her air.

"Ariel from *The Little Mermaid*?" I answered, grinning. She giggled.

It was a dirty laugh as if she was on some secret joke. "So, I see you've already given up your mermaid life to impress a guy you don't even know..." she says, referencing the movie.

"Hah! I know, right? To think of all I sacrificed when I could have just borrowed that breathtaking dress of yours!" She looked quizzically at me as if judging whether I meant my compliment or not.

"Ally." I extended my hand as I introduced myself.

Taking it, she narrowed her eyes. "...You're not in my class, are you?"

"Oh, yeah. Today's my first day and I'm here to collect my subject schedule."

"Year 10th or 11th?"

"11th"

She smiled knowingly.

"Oh, you'll know me soon," she said, and rolled her eyes. I was about to ask her what she meant by that, when a chubby man, most probably in his early fifties, walked in. He was wearing a habit like the Catholic priests wear but surprisingly, sported a mullet. I stood up, while the gorge-girl sprawled even further on her chair until she noticed me.

Then, she smirked, "Noob."

"Now, Daciana, are those the values we learn here?" asked Fr Navindu.

Hmm… so her name was Dah-tchya-na. Was that Ukrainian?

"So, you must be…" Fr Navindu checked a clipboard on his desk. "...Aaliah Zu?"

"Yes, Father."

"Okay, Aaliah, give me a minute and then I shalt set both thee youthful birds free, eh? HAHAH!" boomed Fr Vindu while I smiled weakly and Daciana outright yawned.

"Daciana, please have a seat."

Daciana picked herself up with her devil-may-care attitude and plonked herself down in front of the principal. He squinted at a note on his desk, "Why did you say to Ms. Lo... 'If laughter is the best medicine, your face must be curing the world'?"

Bwahahhha! I liked Daciana already. Wait. Why are both of them looking at me? Did I laugh out loud? Mah-velous. Daciana winked at me and turned towards Fr Vindu, "Why do you keep sending me teachers who are semi-psychotherapists and full psychos?"

Woah, man.

"You will take her morning coffee to her before class, and apologise, Daciana." Fr Vindu told her in a no-nonsense tone.

"Whatever."

"Also, escort Aaliah to her first class which she seems to be attending with you," said Fr Vindu, handing me a printed timetable card.

"What are our teachers like, Daciana?" I asked as I followed her through the corridors.

"What do you expect, they're so ugly that they scare the crap out of toilets."

Mah-velous. "Oh, except I see that you're taking Economics ...Mr Mak looks like an older Thomas Rhett, if you have a thing for country boys."

I made a face. Daciana smiled. "Don't you have any other classes with me?"

"Ally, you're new here so you should know, I'm not someone you want to be seen hanging out with."

What? "Why?"

"Because I'm a prick. The teachers as well as the students will automatically assume you're one too."

"SO? Daciana, I see that you're a bit persuasive but I will do as I please, thank you very much. You cannot dictate me."

Daciana sighed hard and some of her tousled blonde hair lifted up before softly falling back into place. Man, and here was my hair, stringy scarlet noodles.

The classrooms at St. Regis Ruler were airy cubical rooms with white tiled floors and half blue walls decorated with cloud-patterned wallpapers. The teacher's desk faced the door so you couldn't sneak out, and one wall had a row of windows which looked out on the street. Two students shared one desk, sitting on separate black plastic chairs.

I followed Daciana to the first desk in the row of window seats, which seemed like a dark corner because the windows started from the seat right behind it. Daciana slumped into one of the chairs and immediately put her head down on the tattooed desk. As I hung my bag over the other chair, she examined me with her eyebrows furrowed. "Dude, you already look cracked with those fiery red drapes, do yourself a favour and don't spell it out for them by sitting here with me."

I took a quick glance around. Sure enough, almost the whole class, which had about thirty students, was inspecting me. I waved a little with a pan-faced smile, causing some of them to look away and awkwardly return to their business, while others just giggled. A few guys, I noticed, waved back and one bearded fella winked.

Huh. Okay. I planted myself on my seat after a short balding man entered the class and greetings were exchanged. Daciana promptly closed her eyes and drifted off. A few minutes into the lecture, his eyes finally found me. "...including individual agents and markets, their interactions, and the outcomes of interact—YOU!"

I mimicked his expression with raised eyebrows and widened eyes, waiting. Composing himself he finally said, "...must be the new student! Please come here and introduce yourself to us."

Mah-velous. Ok, calm down. Just say your name and a cheerful phrase. I walked towards the teacher's table and faced the class. Smirking mouths and arched eyebrows regarded me with interest. "Uh. Hi, I'm Ally Zu and..." I cannot tell them where I'm from or they might figure out my connection to my dad. Think, Ally, think! Should I tell them my hobbies? I love alternative rock, literary fiction, and solving graph circles! Um.

"...And she told me that she's excited to be with you all!" came a voice from my right. Daciana.

"Yes!" I beamed at her gratefully. "It's nice to meet you!" I said to the class. Some students nodded while the bearded weirdo and another skinhead murmured something in approval.

As I sat down, I just knew I liked Daciana. Soon after, the bell rang and Daciana walked with me to my next class for Political science.

"The Anthropology class will be on the 2nd floor, kay? D'ya need me to meet you near the stairwell?"

"Yes, Daciana, if that's no problem."

Raising her eyebrows and parting her curvy lips, she said, "*I* won't be the one having problems, mind you. Make new friends, Ally."

She turned at the last word, and walked off in the opposite direction to her Education science class. Okay. Let's hope I find Daze or Edie here or even Caecilia would do. I already look strange enough without having to sit alone.

Walking in, my eyes scanned the room for a vacant seat. Okay, there it was in the column beside the window seat. Quite a few gazes were on me by now. A buzzcut skinny guy sat on the table with his feet on the chair, rapping in some foreign language to an audience of five or six people.

I politely paused two steps away, waiting for him to finish before I asked for the seat but moments later, his audience was giving *me* the once-over. Sure enough, he got distracted and stopped midway to look at me warily. "...Oh, hi! That sounded mah-velous! Do you mind if I sit here? I'm Ally and—"

"Nope."

That was pretty direct. Well, I can always *make* him let me sit there through Zaekhuru, but not in front of this audience. I'll just have to—anyway, not on the first day, Ally, or you'll have to run from this state too.

"...Okay, but may I ask why?"

A guy from his audience, wearing a Hawaiian shirt answered, "Because missy, we don't entertain the kith and kin of that *Idiohchiana*."

My clueless expression made another one of the audience members, this time a tomboy girl, speak up, "He means Daciana, missy Sue-tupid." So, this was what Daciana had warned me about. I'd have to ask her why this prejudice existed, because she was cool and friendly in my opinion. I turned around, since I had to have the final word, "I just *thought* y'all were blockheads until you opened your mouths and proved it." I heard someone snigger but didn't dare look back.

Now what? Where do I sit? I scrutinised the other rows with my head low. Ummm... THERE! Last table, window seats column, beside that guy—

...SHIKERDOODLES. MAN, one tasty guy. He was detachedly slumped on the chair near the window, his arm around the vacant chair beside him, his legs spread out in pale grey jeans that naturally faded at the knees.

The last time I saw hair like his was Brad Pitt in *A River Runs Through It*, except this dude's were slightly askew instead of Brad's silky straight blond, like he'd just combed his fingers through it after a shower. His dark baggy denim jacket couldn't hide how well his black T-shirt fit his solid torso. His head was a little upward, focusing nowhere in particular as he scrunched his flawless forehead in thought. By some stroke of luck for me, he was sitting alone.

Okay, Ally! Time to put out—uh, I mean put on your best self.

I tried to smooth my frizzy hair, straightened my dress, and walked confidently to him. He was still engrossed in his thoughts and didn't notice me standing beside the table. Up close, I discovered that his hair was bleached; he was a brunette like me. This has to be fate!

"Hey." I smiled my ToBT smile.

His eyeballs shifted to my face, while the rest of him didn't move at all. He had very blanched brown irises, almost amber, so intense that they seemed to penetrate my skin. "Hi—" Shikerdookies, Ally, how many times are you going to greet him?

...Oh, now he's parted those plump lips. Man, I wonder how soft those lips would feel if you touched them. "Hello, uhhh—"

THIRD TIME NOW. ALLY! COME ON!

"—Is this seat taken?" I finally managed to say, flashing my ToBT smile again.

His frown hadn't changed. He was still staring at me, my face, like I might be a threat. His almost amber eyes made me want to look at them forever, but that might be harmful. I found myself blushing and I broke eye contact to behold his biceps instead. Hmm... just a little sinewy and not totally bulky—the best kind. Definitely not steroidal.

Wait, are my eyes glazing over? ALLY! GET AHOLD OF YOURSELF. I blinked a few times, and realised that he still hadn't moved an inch or said a word.

There might be a possibility that this Foxyguy is high. Or what if he's deaf? Yeah, that must be it! I widened my eyes and pointed at myself with my index finger, then pouted as I pointed to the chair. (Why did I pout?) ..Now, how do you demonstrate 'sit'?

I turned a bit so that he could see my butt and for good measure, wiggled it as if adjusting on the seat. Heard one or two hushed laughs somewhere from the rapper's audience. Mah-velous. Expecting Foxyguy to bolt off protecting his sanity, I returned to my original position, my face the picture of an apology.

He was still frowning but his forehead was less scrunched up now and his lips were pressed together… in amusement I hope, not to smother an internal scream.

"…Who… are you?" His voice was deep and appealing, like a breathy Jared Leto.

I smiled ToBT again. "I'm Ally."

Best to stop here.

"Okay… and you are twerking in my face because…"

HEY! THAT WASN'T TWERKING! Wait, was it? Looks like he's about to shoo me away with more mean comments like the rapper.

"Because you were examining me like I was the first ever cloned sheep instead of answering whether I could sit here or not!"

His frown returned. "I sit alone."

"Well, there's no other chair left and you don't own this table so I'm just gonna—" Sometimes, you have to fend for yourself, no matter how attractive your opponent is. I perched my previously-twerking butt on the chair.

Foxyguy immediately snatched his arm away, as if I was on fire. Huh. Then he leaned closer. His eyebrows were bushy, but arched. He pursed his lips as if abstaining from being surprised.

"I SIT ALONE." He spoke almost in a whisper but with menace.

OK. Was it just me or did Foxyguy look hot this angry? For a second, I just inhaled through my mouth because it seemed like my nose couldn't take in enough air at once which would be required for me to not hyperventilate. Okay. Foxyguy was not going to budge. I'll have to go *there* now. I gingerly locked eyes with him and concentrated, willing him to let me sit there.

I am a Zaekhuru like my father. I discovered it when I was 8, during an oral test when the teacher was punishing those who were unable to answer. As she reached my desk, I simply looked into her eyes and willed with all my innocent heart that she refrains from asking me. She froze, as if in thought for two seconds, and blinked in confusion. Then she walked over to the next seat. I was the only one in the class who had escaped the test.

I tried it again the next week when my maths teacher discovered that I'd calculated a sum wrong. He started berating me in front of the whole class, but before he could say much I held his gaze and willed him to let me go.

"AGAIN YOU HAVE MESSED UP HERE ALLY, I'M TELLING YOU IF—" he trailed off and blinked at me. Then he checked the other sums silently and handed me my notebook.

Needless to say, this type of repetitive behaviour didn't go unnoticed by the students and soon enough, they started talking.

Some feared me; some thought I practised witchcraft, while a few even assumed I was from another planet. They started calling me names like psycho, Dementor, and so forth. My friends started excluding me from their lives, even though I had stopped using my ability right after the first comment was made. Obviously, a school transfer was in line.

St. Regis Ruler was the third school I transferred to.

There were good times too. The hottest guys asked me out, either by their own will or by mine if I wanted. I would be lying if I said I didn't use this ability to get small discounts on branded clothes.

Dad had warned me never to reuse it on a single person in a short span of time because consequent memory gaps will not only affect their life but may also give *me* away. His first advice had been to avoid it unless necessary. And that's what I did.

C'mon, Foxyguy. Let me be. We eyeballed each other for only about three seconds, but it must have felt like minutes to him. Then I blinked and broke eye contact. Foxyguy narrowed his eyes. "Have I seen you somewhere?"

Man. This happened sometimes as an aftereffect of *hipnozes njerezore* aka HiN. Confusion, disorientation or buzzing were common. I settled comfortably on the chair as the teacher entered. Foxyguy stared at me some more before shifting his chair a few centimetres away and tilting his head upwards, with the same crease in his forehead and eyes glazed.

Hiding behind my ample frizzy hair, I regarded his black espadrilles-clad feet and his left wrist resting on his left thigh. His fingers looked firm but skin soft, with little wisps of silky hair on the back of his palm. I had an urge to feast my eyes upon his torso again and slowly, I turned my head away.

OH! HE WAS GAZING AT ME. Well, it was more of a glare but at least I had held his attention. "What's *your* name?" I asked him.

He sighed and tilted his head backwards again. Man, what's *with* him? Does he *have* to be this obnoxious? Anyway, enough wasting my energy on making out—uh, making friends with obnoxiousfoxyguy. Let's concentrate on governance systems.

So, not just the rapper and his audience, but many random students were looking at me—well, both obnoxiousfoxyguy and me—exchanging looks while the teacher continued explaining. Promptly enough, the bell rang, and it was now time for my Psychology class.

TWO

As I started walking away, I decided to have one last look at him and turned abruptly. Unfortunately, he was walking quite close behind me so we ended up almost colliding. Standing up, he looked even more striking, with my head just reaching his lips. I could see his chest rise and fall. I shyly looked up to find him staring at me expressionlessly with those intense eyes.

NOPE, I couldn't. This stare-war wasn't going to happen. Breathing out an "excuse me," I quickly walked towards the exit. I'd already given up the temporary resolution I'd made to avert using HiN to solve my problems but what else was I supposed to do?

And what was the deal with obnoxiousfoxyguy anyway? I might not be as beautiful as Daciana, but I'm not ugly either. My ex used to say that I look like a round-faced version of the girl who played the lead in the Disney show *iCarly* and I've received my fair share of "cuuuuute" comments on social media.

Another one of my strengths is politeness (though fake). What else? Umm I think I have a decent butt, thanks to squats. I've also adopted the practice of being kind to animals because they are so much better than humans. I'm kinda social—SOMEONE IS TOUCHING MY SHOULDERS—"ooooh Ally-lala!" It's Daze SINGING... Man.

Why are guys here attacking me with their gorgeousness? Daze is such a hunk with that smile to die for and he's so good-natured over that! He walked with me, his hand still on my shoulder.

"Any issues yet, Ally?"

I smiled at him. "Nothing I can't handle."

"HAH, that's good! Where're you heading to now?"

"Psychology, and you?" Daze grinned, SHIKERDOODLES... ask me out already, man.

"I knew you and I had a similar destination to end up at."

I rolled my eyes at him, smiling, but actually I was very much relieved that I won't have to search for a seat in this class at least. We entered the class and Daze walked over to the second row from the windows, taking the second desk, where a man in dreads was sitting already. "Hey Lendrick, man."

Cue man-shoulder kiss. "My man Daze, alright?"

Then his gaze shifted to me. "Whom do I have the pleasure of meeting here..."

He extended his hand. I smiled at him and shook his hand. "I'm Ally."

"Hey Ally. Are you in our class?"

"Yeah, Lendrick."

"Lendrick, man, would you mind letting Ally—" Daze gently thumped the table.

Lendrick made an 'O' with his lips and nodded, winking at Daze and picking up his bag to move to the back. ...Okay.

"After you, m'lady." Daze curtseyed. Man, he's so cute.

A horde of pretty girls kept shooting me looks, which, let's be honest, I totally deserved. It was clear that Daze was the class hunk from the way the girls vied for his attention. Some flicked their hair when they greeted him, others touched his shoulder as they passed, and then there were some who even touched his T-shirt.

Daze glowed in their attention, for which he cannot be blamed. Mrs Kaam, our 'psycho' teacher was a blond vixen with curls who was wearing a pink casual flapper dress to teach. Yes, I'm serious. I could see why the guys were greater in strength in this room.

Daze jotted down almost nothing during the whole lecture, but still Mrs Kaam smiled at him when she passed by. If I shot Daze about 9-10 looks throughout the period, I caught him inspecting me for at least half of them.

What was different was how every time I caught him staring, he just smiled sexily instead of looking away. Man, I was getting flustered.

At the bell, Daze wanted to know what my next class was. "Oh, Philosophy? Great, Caecilia will accompany you, c'mon."

Shikerdoodles. Friction, meet my life. I followed Daze through the corridors, noticing how broad his shoulders were. Yum. This view makes up for the crappy things one endures in life. Wait, who's this pulling on his arm? ...Caecilia.

She pulled him aside, holding his right forearm with both hands. It made it apparent that whatever she was whispering to him was not meant for my ears. I waited politely at two-hands distance, trying to appear nonchalant but feeling awkward. She's shooting me censorious looks while widening her eyes at Daze. What's with her? Ho-hum, my thighs feel cold standing out here.

Now Daze is nodding. He turns to face me, not quite meeting my eyes. Noticing my cue, I walk toward them, raising my eyebrows in inquiry.

"Ally, uh... Caecilia heard that you sat with Daciana in the first class... Did you?"

Not this again! "Uh, yeah I did, Daze. Why?"

"Um, Ally—"

"BECAUSE Daciana is not a virtuous girl!" Caecilia spat, cutting off Daze.

Virtuous? What are we? The Sisters Of Our Holy Ramen? Who uses that word anyway?

"Who says that?" I asked.

Daze appeared uncomfortable.

"Daciana's reputation is that of an abusive alcoholic, do you know that?" hissed Caecilia.

Woah. How was she the judge of deciding what reputation was acceptable? Why should the society dictate someone's conscience? Wait. Why was Caecilia now opening and closing her mouth like a fish. Oh, she's taken aback by something… OH. I SPOKE OUT LOUD AGAIN. Well, I didn't say anything wrong.

Daze looked like he wanted to be anywhere else but here. "But you've not heard her speak yet! She shouldn't abuse as much as she does. It makes all of us women look crass!" Caecilia whined.

"Which neurotic dictated how women should be? If being bold and loud doesn't make the men look lousy, why should it reflect poorly on women, Caecilia? Every person is different. Maybe you have been brought up in a socially-abiding and patriarchal atmosphere, but I have been raised to be cannier and daring. This does not make me less of a woman than you are, Caecilia."

I hope I wasn't sounding as agitated as I felt, so I added her name as a measure of relaxation. Caecilia chewed her lower lip and looked thoughtful.

An awkward silence prompted Daze to tap Caecilia's shoulder and ask her to be with me in class. Caecilia mutely nodded, still zoned out. Then she observed me warily for a few seconds before tilting her head towards the classroom, pressing her lips together and walking ahead. I took that as an intimation to follow her. Caecilia put her bag down on the table right in front of the teacher's desk. Shikerdoodles. She was a geek. After settling in, she turned to me with those puppy dog eyes.

"Ally, I've known Daze since we played in sand pits. I've been with him through his Moccasins phase and helped him transition to sneakers. His favourite meal—basil and Tofu Ramen—was invented by me! Try all you want, but your Kawaii Tsundere crap will not change our nine years together."

...Ugh man, Daze wore Moccasins once? I blinked at her patronisingly.

"Copyright that ramen meal then, Caecilia, because very soon he might be eating out of my hands."

Bring it on. Caecilia gasped, but before she could think of a reply, the old teacher walked in. Mr Laabh was an almost hairless senior citizen who asked a lot of questions in class. After my introduction, he immediately jumped in with, "So Ms Zu, I'll help you catch up. Last week, we discussed creation and existence. Where do you think we came from?"

Okay, so my appearance always makes people assume I'm a callous and impulsive bimbo, but if I find something interesting, I perform well. So let's see… existence. Should I explain it scientifically or theologically? Thank god I read.

"Well, I like the explanation from the African traditions, that only water, darkness and one great god existed before us. One day, God experienced a tummy-ache and vomited up what we now know as the Sun. The sun dried up some of the water and land came into existence. But God was still not done vomiting—" I heard some chuckles. "—so next, God threw up the moon, the stars, the gorillas, the dogs, the tigers… and finally, here I am standing before you."

I finished with a flourish, sneaking a peek at the amused faces of my peers and a beaming Mr Laabh. My reverie was interrupted by a little hand waving near my chin.

"A first-rate try, Ms. Zu, yes, Ms. Yaasik?"

Caecilia Yaasik. Okay.

"Mr Laabh, that was clearly a myth."

Oh, how dare she? She was definitely a product of someone throwing up.

"Around 80 years ago, Hubble discovered that the galaxies are moving away from us, which raised the debate that, at one point of time, they must have been close to us. The steady state theory suggested that the universe would have existed forever and would have looked the same at all times—"

I zoned out around here, and so did some other students, evident from the buzz in the back and the screen glow of the phones held in some hands.

Caecilia's constant attempts to compete with me in everything, even as elementary as one's speed of taking notes, or trying to sit up straighter to appear taller beside me (huh, nice try, shortie), are amusing. She also hunches over her phone while furiously texting, clearly trying to hide the screen from me. Yeah, yeah, botch all you want about me to your little friends. Nothing would dissuade me from snatching the loosely-held Daze away from your clasp. I am bored by the time the bell rings for lunch break.

Following Caecilia will take me to where Daze and his friends gather for lunch. There is mad hysteria as kids run about in the corridors, some even pausing in my way and gaping at my hair as I pass by, flashing them a sarcastic smile. Jeez, I resent kids. Why do they yell so much? I have a theory that their yelling is their default volume, and their whispering is actually their general voice.

Shuddering at this thought, I notice we have moved away from the mainstream crowded areas now. Daze and Bulkyboy are standing near the big electric generator at one of the corners in the field.

Man, why do guys inhale food through their mouths and call it eating? I wish I hadn't seen gorgeous Daze compromised like this, with some kinda schezwan sauce coating his lips. Fadil is munching on a bulging wrap, and he catches Caecilia's eyes first, giving her a toothy smile when he discovers that the freshly sealed box she holds contains dry mushroom chilli.

With some anticipation, those same eyes wander to the packed soup tumbler in my hand and the light in them diminishes visibly. I roll my eyes inwardly as I give a small, fake smile to a disgruntled Caecilia, who has just realised that I've been walking one step behind her this whole time. She thought she'd lose me in the crowd.

"Awliowhhh."

Gosh! Can Daze chew before he feels the need to speak and butcher my name like that! (Although, it doesn't change the fact that his irises and hair colour match perfectly, what a beauty).

"Hhow was your forst hhalf? ...hey arr you just guhnna dronk souhp for lunch?" He finally swallows what seems like half of his lunch in one go. Casting a glance at a frowning Caecilia, who didn't even get a look of acknowledgement from Daze (tee hee), I answer, "Hi Daze, yeah 10 minutes more of school is all I can bear for today. Goodnight."

We continue to whine about the faculty until Edie joins us with her Manchurians from the canteen and directs me towards where I can find hot water for my soup. The canteen is a mock hut-shaped room where they have a few dishes ready to serve from oven compartments at one side of the wall, snack packets on another and a refrigerator and hot water dispenser at the third perpendicular.

It is remarkably crowded and I think I spot Foxyguy's messy blond mop but can't pursue my line of gaze if I want to drink the soup out of my cup and not through sucking the front of my sweater dress.

I spot Daciana sitting, poking around at her tofu dish, flanked by two very shady-looking guys and one girl who seems semi-high, I wave at her. She considers me for a second before passing me a genuine smile. I can tell still is trying to discourage me from being friendly with her.

How can she be such an outcast when she is so kind that she is able to show compassion even towards a stranger like me?

"...and dahdy legit saihd that he will buy it for me but then I'll hafto consider it as my birthday gift for this year!" Fadil is incredulously booming as I reach them.

"High five on still being treated like a twelve year old, Fadil." Caecilia squints at Fadil's palm touching mine.

She then shoots an intense look at Edie, probably to see if she's as affected by this simple gesture as much as Caecilia herself is. Edie is lost elsewhere, staring out at the activity in the college grounds.

"Hey Edie, which class do you have next?"

Jerked out of her reverie, she answers, "Sociology."

"What, that's mah-velous! What's the faculty like?"

"He dyes his hair. And his moustache. Burgundy," she monotones.

Indeed, Mr Rachit not only has a lush burgundy head and facial hair, but also a tie to match. I make my way to the back benches of the second column from the windows. Before I plant my tush, I get the feeling that someone is smiling at me from the last bench. My eyes meet a very eye-catching girl who wears a blue turban around her herringbone braids and has three piercings in one ear and none on the other. Her smile is wide and I find my own matching its ardour.

"Hi Gabby! I saw you near Union medicals yesterday, do you live there or something?" gushes Edie.

Woah, Edie is smiling. She knows how to smile.

"Yeah, I *do* live there, Edie! What were you doing there? And don'tchu dare enter my place without asking my momma's permission or she gon' beat you arse all the way back to your own bedroom! Hahaa!"

Gabby turns to me again. "Hellooo, have we met before? I'm Gabby Harris, and gurrrl, I love that weave!"

"Oh? It's natural but thank you! My name is Aaliah and today's my first day here." I'm pretty sure I've got anime eyes right now.

"Say what? That's original? May I?" She extends her hand towards my locks and examines them. Satisfied by what she felt, she smiles brightly at me again.

"If your shampoo goes missing sometime soon, *I* finna won't be the one who's stolen it!" We giggle in harmony as Edie bursts into laughter. Throughout the class, Gabby's amusing remarks make us giggle. It amazes me how freely Edie laughs, almost like she's a different person altogether. By the end of the class, I've exchanged numbers with Gabby. Edie nudges me and copies it from my phone almost immediately, but secretly. She's a little weird.

Unfortunately, he's the first object my eyes land on as I walk into my History classroom. Shikerdoodles man, he's laid back against one of the chairs, second column last seat, and his legs are crossed at the ankles, up on the desk.

His body stance is at ease but there's an immobile frown on his face which compliments his overcast eyes, scanning... infinity. His T-shirt clings smoothly to the curve of his shoulders and fits him perfectly across his chest. The hand which isn't draped across his seat is absentmindedly caressing his blonde tufts at the back of his head.

It really sucks that the bizarre people are the most beautiful ones. I cannot seem to look away and soon enough, as if he heard some telepathic call, his eyes crawl up to meet mine. His expression doesn't change but everything around me seems to slow down. I know I am still walking inside the class ...somewhere… he's getting closer… WHY CAN'T I LOOK AWAY... or rather why can't HE look away!? Neither of us smiles, or nods, or shows any form of acknowledgement. It's just plain eerie!

"Ally! Hi! You want a seat?" A gruff voice on my left pulls me out of this impromptu blinking battle.

It's late but I realise I'm standing right in front of Foxyguy AND he is still scrutinising me with the slight frown. I narrow my eyes at him before turning towards the deep voice, which belongs to Fadil. Oh, thank god, he's sitting on the column adjacent to Foxyguy's, so it does not look like he was the one I heedlessly made my way towards.

"Yes, Fadil, that would be mah-velous," I coo as I slide into the neighbouring chair.

Fadil smells like sweat and saplings, like a human greenhouse. I lean away from him a little too often during the lecture. The third time I do that, I turn my head to look centrifugally at Foxyguy. No surprises—he's squinting at me like he has just figured out that I part time as a flamingo bird. I shoot him a scowl, and thereafter try to concentrate on the class.

Needless to say, the whole time I feel like he might be staring at me. Just to play safe, I play with my hair a bit, sit straight and keep my legs crossed—NO I DON'T HAVE AN EXPLANATION FOR THIS OKAY? LEAVE ME ALONE.

The History teacher, Mr Ira, a jovial and easygoing folk, calls me to his desk for a personal introduction at the very end when the bell rings. He makes small talk and tells me to make "many friends". Wow, great advice, Mr Ira, I'll make sure to do that, otherwise my HiN would. I walk back to my desk, looking around to see the classroom almost completely empty except for Foxyguy who was dozing off on his seat, head against the wall. His face looks serene now that he is no longer frowning. His locks flop over his eyebrow and his mouth is ajar. I can see the ends of his two front teeth.

I slide back into my seat to gather my notebook when I hear Mr Ira address Foxyguy.

"SNAP out of your dream, Mr Juhnson."

Oh? Juhnson. Lol. He doesn't look like a Juhnson though, more like a ...Castle or a ...um... Grimes or something. Needless to say, Mr Ira *snaps* Foxyjuhnson out of his slumber. He gets up and starts walking slowly but steadily. I blink at his small tight butt and admire how his jeans fit him like a second skin.

Cursing at how I am unable to find the perfect denims that would hug my bottoms this well without scrunching up at weird contortions, I get up only to cry out and fall back down.

Shikerdoodles. A lock of my hair is probably caught on some spare screw jutting out of the bench.

I can neither see it, nor reach back to untangle it.

The classroom is empty now and I'm panicking. I try to pull my head but it's a big lock and I don't wanna end up with a bloody bald patch on my first day, man! My worried eyes meet Foxyjuhnson's confused ones. He is standing near the vacant teacher's table, facing the door as he's about to leave. We don't say anything as I continue to tug at my hair which will NOT UNLODGE!!!

THIS IS SO EMBARASSING. Should I pretend like I'm listening to music and nodding my head? I try that but the pain on my distorted face apparently gives me away. Foxyjuhnson visibly sighs and everything but drags himself toward my seat. Tens of possibilities fill my brain. Maybe he'll flip me and walk off. Maybe he'll stamp on my shoe, call me a supreme tosser, and walk off.

"Are you unable to bail it out?" he asks me in a bored voice. Mortified, I nod, wincing as this motion pulls on the tangled locks.

Suddenly his legs are straddling my seat. He's reaching over behind me to check where my hair is stuck. And my face is inches away from his crotch. Yes. This sums up my life. I try shallow breathing, my mind numbed by the situation and not wanting to anticipate what might happen if either of us moves an inch. I feel one or two quiet tugs on my head and let out an 'ow' louder than necessary so that he realises where my mouth is.

"Hm. This isn't going to come off easy."

What? His jeans? Oh, my hair.

Jeez. His hand reaches inside the opposite arm of his jacket and then, to my utter horror, he pulls out a dagger.

A WHAT.

The dagger has a wooden butt, and the place where the blade fits into the handle is literally shaped like a butt. That butt makes me realise how I'm in a room alone with a strange (but hot) guy, stuck, unable to move AND he is armed with a dagger. I am one of those potentially foolish girls you hear on TV about when your aunt baloney says, "Ah, this dumb fudge nugget had it coming." NO. I bolt upright, butt and all.

He pauses. Of course, he has to; my forehead is practically colliding with his lips. Blushing furiously, I take in the proximity of his arms encasing my body, though not touching me. Too shocked to look up to his eyes, I catch myself staring at his neck.

The ends of his collarbone jut out, gorgeously escaping the round neck of his dark tee. His Adam's apple is not too prominent; the skin at the side of his neck is clear and smooth. My first instinct is to imagine how warm my lips would feel against it (Don't ask why).

In a matter of two seconds, I observe laterally that he has tensed too, though I'm pretty sure he isn't looking at my neck, not that he would be able to, with me being tiny in front of his six-foot self. Carefully, I tilt my face upwards, the restriction from my hair making the movement difficult, to gauge his reaction.

I know my eyes must be wide because I'M FREAKING OUT. WHY DON'T THEY HAVE THOSE SELF-HELP BOOKS ON HOW TO REACT IN CLOSE SPACES WITH FOXYJUHNSONS!? Uh-oh, he's frowning slightly at something but his lips are parted and uhhh, he's blinking rapidly.

Suddenly I hear a *chink* and my head jerks forward, my forehead touches his jawline. As I gasp, with lightning speed, a lock of scarlet hair dangles before my eyes. My eyes grow as big as UFOs, darting from my disembodied hair to his vain, tight-lipped face.

It sinks in that his arms are no longer around me, so I gingerly lift my fingers to grab my—*sob*—beautiful but disobedient hair from his grasp. He lets it go as soon as I touch it as if it's caught fire. Huh. Do I disgust him?

He extracts himself from our 'cozy' position and walks away as I stare in disbelief at the lock of hair which once belonged to my head. I'll definitely have to tie it up from tomorrow. Well, how many of you can confidently say that the guy you have the hots for has given you a haircut? Huh? Man. I'm already late for my anthropology class, maybe I should make a run for it. Eh, the faculty is a short, stumpy woman who's glaring at my tardy self over her glasses.

"So YOU are the new girl, ay? Is this what they allowed at your old school? Clown-like colourful hair, snooty expressions, walking into classes anytime you like, ay? Wh—"

"Excuse me, ma'am? Ally left her glasses in the canteen at lunch, maybe that's why she had trouble finding her way to the classroom."

The voice belongs to Daciana who's waving a pair of thick black half-rimmed spectacles which I am seeing for the first time in my life.

"...OH you found them, Daciana! Goodness gracious, thank you! I'm sorry, madam. Actually I am not yet familiar with these hallways—as I AM the new girl, you see, I had to peer closely at a number of classrooms before I found this one." I make a puppy dog face and blink an unnecessary amount of times.

As the class progresses, I relax with Daciana and thank the force of karma or whatever, for letting me escape the wrath of this mini-dictator. We're sitting at the front but the teacher is standing in the middle of the room so she pretty much has her back towards us.

Daciana nudges me and gestures her head towards a guy in the other row. I follow her gaze. A lean Clark Kent look-alike with glasses is absorbed in the lecture, jotting important bullet points in his notepad. I meet Daciana's eyes and mouth "Daddy." She makes an I-told-you-so face.

"Is he your boyfriend?" I whisper.

"Dude. I wish."

"Is he single?"

He must be passionately smitten elsewhere if he doesn't find Daciana hot.

"No, much worse—he's a prude... I guess."

Now that she has pointed it out, I notice it too. He's wearing gel in his combed and side-parted hair and actually has trousers on instead of denims like the general population. My eyes return to the hot mess that is Daciana, with her tousled tresses and smudged eyeshadow.

"Have you guys talked?"

Daciana considers me with tired eyes before recounting how she once tried to have a conversation with him about an assignment and how he'd squinted at her with a scowl like she had crawled out of the gutter and still had crap stuck to her face.

Daciana and I have exchanged numbers by the time the class ends. I am happy that she's let go of that 'don't-hang around-me-chile' vibe. Surprisingly, Daze is waiting for me outside the classroom. Daciana distances herself immediately and walks away, but not before shooting me a little wave which I return eagerly.

Daze's gaze is on me and I find myself instantly blushing. Most of the girls passing by are checking him out appreciatively and some of them are even following his tunnel vision towards me.

We walk along and I tell him excitedly about how Daciana saved me from a verbal lashing, carefully omitting out the part about why I was late. He smiles and nods before adding, "So you've picked out a BFF for yourself, huh? No chance for me?"

FUDGE NUGGETS, HE'S SO KYOT. "Oh c'mon, do you hate me that much?"

He gives me a playful, almost pleading smile. I think of something clever to say which cancels out friendzoning but doesn't come on too strong.

"If I hated you, would I have asked Santa for you this Christmas?" I flutter my eyelashes (I AM SORRY LADIES—I KNOW THIS WAS CRINGY AS HECK BUT YOU WEREN'T THE ONES DEALING WITH THE DESSERT THAT DAZE IS).

Our commerce faculty is a bespectacled stout young woman who is very interactive and likes to joke around. When someone arrives late, she allows him in without any questions asked.

"Oh, 'late Mr Juhnson' is here."

Haha the pun. 'Late.' Wait.

WHOMST. ARE YOU SERIOUS? HOW MANY CLASSES DO I HAVE WITH FOXYJUHNSON!? He walks inside frowning and happens to catch my eye. His frown deepens as he holds my gaze as long as possible until he passes me to sit at the last seat in the column where I'm sitting. When I turn my head to face the front again, Daze is staring at me curiously. Uh oh.

"That guy… he's a weirdo. He's a loner too. Why do the loners always catch your eyes, huh?"

Okay, Daze is giving me his super CUTE side grin. Mmmmm. The rest of the lecture goes smoothly. I'm careful to not look at FoxyJuhnson again, lest Daze should get suspicious and feel like I'm interested in him and therefore, back away in some weird bro-code.

Before I know it, the bell rings. All I can think about is my head hitting the fluffy blue pillows on my soft blue bed, the huge windows, and drifting off to dreamland (while doing some homework, sadly).

Daze seems to have some other plans in mind. His gang—Caecilia, Fadil and Edie—joins us, appearing out of nowhere, as we head towards the main gate. I am caught off-guard by an enthusiastic Caecilia literally jumping arse-first onto Daze's motorcycle while it's still parked.

The fudge nugget is up? When she sees Daze's set jaw and her smug smile fades, I can sense her chagrin. Still waiting for someone to explain what is going on, I sneak a peek at Daze, only to find him regarding me sheepishly.

"Yeah, Ally, would you mind sitting between Caecilia and me?"

Immediately, Caecilia starts to protest, but Daze gently raises a palm without looking at her. Um. Is everyone coming to Daze's place? So much for my nap.

"Is… that even allowed?"

I am not well-versed with the handbook of the road lurkers but I know enough that three teens on a two-seater is not legal. Also, I don't want Caecilia sitting behind me and staring at my butchered lock for twenty minutes. Daze has the decency to look timid as his hand caresses the back of his head.

"There's no other way—" He's half smiling as he starts, but Caecilia interrupts with a quiet snarl, "You see, Ally, it used to be allowed when it was just the four of us originally, but now you're here too, so there's a problem. A problem of conveyance," she adds, glancing at Daze as he passes her a look.

Ah, this *betch*. I glance at Daze and he's looking at me expectantly. Nah, no way this is going to end like this with them making me break the traffic rules.

"Okay guys, I won't cause problems. I'll call a cab."

Daze is already shaking his head in disagreement. "Caecilia, just come sit behind Edie, don't beh a spoilsport," Fadil quips in a bored voice.

I can almost hear Caecilia snorting and I catch her shooting a pleading look at Daze. Although everyone can see how Daze is ignoring her obvious feelings, she perhaps chooses not to. At this point, I almost feel bad for her. We women always get caught up in situations where we become enemies to each other. Still, as much as I feel for her, I cannot help her plans with Daze. I'm not compromising my principles for anyone.

"How am I being a spoilsport? She's the one who's acting all high and mighty! Why can't you ask HER to not be a *spoilsport*!?"

Fadil cocks an eyebrow at me as if to say, 'Fair enough.' Uh no, I'm not going to start explaining myself to a group of people and then give them another chance to label me as a "prudence angel 101."

"Guys, why can't you just let me get a taxi so we can just go home!" I say, throwing in some unnecessary jazz hands to lighten the mood.

Silent Edie pitches in this time, "Uh, Ally, I think it won't be completely safe for you, given that you aren't familiar with the city yet?"

Shikerdoodles maximus. Daze turns to me. "Ally, I'll drive carefully, I won't let you fall, trust me."

"It's not that I don't trust you, Daze. What you're asking me to do here is illegal because it's dangerous."

Daze turns to Caecilia. "Caecilia, Fadil will drive carefully—"

"OH MY GOD. YOU HAVE GOT TO BE KIDDING ME, DAZE! I've been your best friend since 5th standard! Who IS she that you're compromising our thing for her!?"

An awkward silence ensues.

"Stop making a scene, Caecilia. Don't be stubborn, you—"

"Ah! So now *I'm* the stubborn one but not your *friend* here who looks like Ronald McDonald's first trip to the salon!"

I… okay, but I respect that insult somewhere deep inside.

Fadil is struggling to hold back his smile. Caecilia isn't done yet; she turns to me and says, "Is this what you normally do, Ally? Jump between close friends and ruin their friendships?"

"Caecilia." I took a deep breath to calm myself.

"When did I ever imply that I want to ride with Daze or that I don't want you to ride with him? I'll go with Fadil, but not with another pillion."

"Oooh, and why is that, Madam? Your majesty is too suave to sit with me, a commoner, and risk a scratch on them glossy sneakers. She isn't used to the grit of our suburbs, or maybe she wants to corner our boys all alone—"

"MY FATHER," I snapped, my voice rising without meaning to.

"My father was in the police. He gave his life serving the country and always taught me that the rules, the laws, the legislation are there for us to follow. I WILL NOT break the rules for this silly teen drama you think life is for me." Breathing hard, I avoid meeting anyone's eyes.

A few seconds later, I feel a hand on the small of my back. It's Daze, and he's gently guiding me toward his motorcycle. I walk towards it, before turning to gauge Caecilia's reaction.

Her face is flushed, but she's staring at the ground. Fadil is mounting his motorcycle and Edie looks ready to call Caecilia. Believe me, I don't want to project myself as the weak *where-did-my-daddy-go* girl. I try hard to be anything but that, but I didn't want to lie to these people, whom I'll be spending a lot of time with now—Caecilia included.

I don't think she has anything inherently against me, though she does have a gargantuan crush on Daze and I did threaten her jokingly. And yes, I do like Daze, but if he shows even the slightest interest in Caecilia, I'll extract myself from the situation faster than you can spell my nickname.

Until then, he's public property.

Daze and I leave first, followed by Fadil and the girls. I'm not good with directions, but this looks nothing like the route we took for school. After wildly swinging my head around for a full five minutes, I finally let my curiosity ask the question, "Uhhh Daze? Is this a new road? We didn't use this one in the morning, did we?"

"Yeah, it's not that one, we're not going home… wait! You didn't know? We aren't going home." With growing unease, I manage to utter, "Oh?" "Fadil, the girls, and I hang out at this farmhouse where they keep young horses in training to be racehorses. The keeper knows us so he allows us in if we abide by some basic rules. It's a cool, open grassland, and no one bothers us there."

Okay so we're gonna be horsing around. What about the fact that I'm hungry. On cue, my stomach rumbles, and alarmed, I snatch my hand from Daze's shoulder to cup my stomach as if it had a mouth. Daze turns his neck slightly, "You okay, Ally?"

"Uh, yeah." You cannot explain to most boys why you're hungry when you only had soup for lunch because they'll mock you for being pretentious and caring about your body or having a diet routine.

Daze takes several short-cuts, as I can judge from the alleys we pass. He seems to be in a good mood as well, humming a song I do not recognise. Maybe he enjoys these rides. He does seem like one of those sporty men. After about ten minutes, we stopped in front of a small food shack named 'BurgerOn' which has wooden picnic tables on the pavement.

"Do I dismount here?" It would make complete sense if he just dropped me off in a strange neighbourhood and zoomed away with his friends. Though this area seems too tacky for my tastes.

"Yeah, aren't you hungry, Ally?"

I watch him park the motorcycle as I calculate the amount of critters that may have sacrificed themselves in the oil the burger patties here are fried in, weighing it against the hunger I feel. Inconclusively, I watch Edie, Fadil, and Caecilia pull up. Caecilia still looks subdued, but Fadil looks ready to get some BurgerOns into his system.

"The usual for everyone, right? OH! Ally youh gotta try this, man. This's the best bhurgers youh ever had!" Fadil trips over his tongue enthusiastically as he enters the shack. These burgers are probably as exciting to him as ManU or something. I slide onto the bench beside Edie while I notice Caecilia hurry to sit beside Daze. Yeah whatever, I'm straight in his line of vision which makes me more prominent, so she can sit wherever she wants.

Five minutes later, Fadil enters with a tray in hand, stacked with smaller trays. Edie and I help him place it on the table as he gestures to return and grab others' fill. It's a pretty standard looking burger with a plate of liquid cheese beside it. Are we supposed to pour it over the burger? This is going to be as messy as a fudge nugget and I absolutely cannot let cheese drip down my chin or sauce coat my lower lip in front of the guy I have a crush on. As the gang digs in, I ponder over the consequences of mistakenly getting my wild scarlet tresses dipped into cheese and the colour combination that would form and whether or not it'll suit me.

I watch Daze and Caecilia not giving a care about the world and just chomping greedily. This gives me confidence and I finally decide to dip my burger in the cheese and take a bite. SHIKER-FUDGING-DOOKIESS, IT'S ALL GOOEY AND SOFT AND

SPICY AND A VOLCANO OF TEXTURES IN MY MOUTH. By the time I finish, everyone's waiting for me and Edie laughs as I freeze, sensing their attention.

"I think Ally liked it."

"Ooh I dihd!" I force out without dropping food from my mouth onto her lap. Soon after, we take off again.

THREE

We have paused in front of what seems like a tunnel-shaped hall, its far end opening on the road. The area around it is all green fields with tall fences, which makes it hard to peer inside. It doesn't look like the STD-infested addict's neighbourhood I'd been secretly fearing.

Fadil opens the wooden hinged plank door to the tunnel and walks his bike inside what I can now see is a long warehouse-like structure, full of haystacks to the ceiling with a slender passageway that leads further.

As Daze rumbles the motorcycle inside, I catch a faint whiff of... dung? Are we in a petting zoo?

We dismount as the boys park their motorcycles. I sidle up to Edie and whisper, "WHERE the fudge are we?"

Edie smiles mischievously and clasps my hand as she half-sprints deeper into the haystack chasm. Horses. It's a stable. There are mini compartments with some tall horses. A grey imported horse, a beige one with a shining coat, and a white slender one with a silky mane. It's a plethora of beautiful strong healthy equines. At the end of the fourth set of stalls stands a plump middle-aged man, wearing gloves as he digs into a brown horse's ear.

Mr Blabama trains and manages these race horses for his boss who's a wealthy high-profile guy. His wife is taller than him and well-built with wispy hair. She addresses us like she adores us. I learn that they never had an offspring of their own so they adopted an orphaned child from Uganda, and now she's a vet and works in a metro city.

The Blabamas apparently look forward to seeing Daze and the rest of the group coming here on most afternoons. They like the company of the 'young ones,' as Mrs Blabama puts it while asking me twice already if I'd like to try some of her homemade chocolates (no ma'am, thank you!).

Surprised at the confidence with which I see Fadil attach the riding gear on to the white mare, and the ease with which Edie mounts herself up the black beauty, I disclose to Daze that I have never ridden a horse in my life before, in case he's expecting me to just go along with their cowboy antics. He smiles and asks if I'd want to ride on his horse with him.

I can tell what y'all must be thinking, but I really do not know how to manoeuvre myself, let alone an animal five times my size. I'm still feeling hesitant when the brown four-legged cutie sidles up to me and exhales in my face. I glare up to see Daze mounted and grinning at me sheepishly while extending his hand.

Just then, I happen to turn my head to find Caecilia, in the process of guiding her light brown horse out of the stall, frozen. Her eyes, as wide as saucers, keep darting between Daze and me. I don't know if Daze notices my glance at Caecilia, but he says, "It's either me or Fadil because the girls' horses are young."

Immediately clasping his extended palm, I hoist myself across the equine, behind Daze. It's high. All of us reach the other end of the warehouse, which opens into vast green grassland, stretching as far as the eye can see.

Everyone sets off in different directions. Daze fills me in that Mr Blabama cannot give all these horses the required exercise so he lets them take the animals out for a gallop. It's fun riding like this, especially while the horse is trotting, and for the first time in my life, I silently thank my compact bosom which doesn't allow room for any jiggling business. After a few minutes, Daze warns me to hold on tight because he's about to make the horse (named Secretariat, after his resemblance to the famous race horse) run.

At this point, I'm actually feeling somewhat happy. There's a cute single boy who's interested in me. I'm riding a horse in this beautiful landscape. No one knows about my supernatural abilities. Awesome! My arms go around Daze's waist and I inch a little bit closer to him so my chin touches his shoulder as the horse starts to gain pace. A few seconds later I feel one of Daze's hands on mine.

The greenery makes the breeze cool and pleasant, with the sun not too hot today. Losing track of time is easy when you're relaxed.

Even after Secretariat slows down, Daze's palm stays on mine. His fingers caress the back of my hand time and again, and I'll be lying if I say that it doesn't make something inside me flutter. Before I know it, the shed is back in sight.

Reluctantly, though I try not to show it, I alight. Thankfully, Caecilia isn't back yet to glare at me and pass judgements. I accompany Daze to walk Secretariat back to his stall. After closing the gate, Daze takes my hand as if we've known each other since we were six, and starts strolling toward the field, with me following shyly with a smile.

"Do you like this weather, Ally? Cool but not frigid..."

"Yes, it's always colder at my place. It's bleary there and I never want to willingly leave the bed in the morning."

"...Hhaha... you must look cute in bed...uhm—"

He looks away, and I widen my eyes at him, smiling. “Uh, Daze, thanks for the horse ride. It was a great experience. I can’t believe I’ve never tried it before.”

He squeezes my palm before answering, “Definitely my pleasure, Ally. Hey, there’s Fadil and… Caecilia!” Sure enough, they’re approaching us on their equines.

Caecilia’s eyes stay glued on our clasped hands as she enters the shed. Feeling uncomfortable, I gently try to dislodge my fingers but Daze’s hold is steadfast. It’s not long before it’s time to leave. Caecilia doesn’t speak to either Daze or me in the meantime. She just appears to be contemplating something.

The trip back to Daze’s place is uneventful, but I feel more comfortable with him now. We smile at each other before advancing to our separate rooms. Only then do I realise that my headache, which had dimmed in school and at the farmhouse, has renewed itself.

After a whirlwind of homework, reading, and an attempt to rest, it’s time for dinner. We dig into wholesome chaap and paneer tikka, relishing the hearty meal. Daze is smitten by my mum’s cooking skills, especially the tikka. Get in line, Daze. I can’t tell if it was my imagination, but I seemed to catch his eyes on me every time he licked his lips. Then he smirked. Mr Keberkil noticed my blush at one instance and I quickly waved it off as a “reflection of my red hair on my face.”

When I lay down to sleep, memories flood my thumping head. Mum discovered my HiN when I was six years old. I was making my friend Emma play my favourite roleplay game of police and robbers again and again. Once, she even refused in front my mother, who says I held her by her shoulders and peered into her eyes for a few seconds. After that, Emma played along without saying a word.

My mother later asked me what I had been doing at that time, and I'd told her I'd been mentally ordering Emma to play the game.

Poor Emma. She most probably does not remember what happened when we played. I cannot recall how many innocent kids I must have tricked like this before my father sat me down and had the talk with me. He passed away a year later. The guilt that fills me for my actions, even though I was a child, has stayed with me. It makes me realise how everything comes with a price.

My sleep is full of nightmares about Daze lost in the farmhouse, where I could hear him but not find him. When my alarm rings in the morning, I'm still experiencing dullness and heaviness in my head.

It's been 24 hours, and things are beginning to come into perspective for me. Yes, by "perspective" I mean the headache. It's raining. I decided my outfit wisely today and wore my black jeans and tank paired with a fuzzy cream cardigan. This way, I won't have to worry about my dress hiking up while riding a horse and my expensive sneakers getting muddy at the insides (hello, ugly vegan rubber sandals).

Although my scarlet hair goes well with cream, I've not forgotten the FoxyJuhnson sponsored ad-hoc haircut, so I've tied it into a classic bun. Hmm, too plain jane, maybe a fake gold rope chain will do the trick.

Daze widens his eyes at me on the breakfast table. He's in a baby pink polo and looks very clean. Suddenly I feel I look too bleary. Andrea is wearing a babydoll nightie over slacks, and I give her a small smile as we set the breakfast table together. She loudly sings "Having one of those difficult days, Alleeee?"

What the heck are difficult days? Every day is a difficult day for me. Wait—she means periods. Oh fudge nuggets, do I look like Bloody

Mary now? It's even worse that she belted this out in front of Daze who's trying not to appear too engaged but is definitely listening, because who stares so pointedly at a bowl of yoghurt like that?

Mum comes to my rescue, "Ally dislikes the rain so she's just trying not to get goosebumps and keep herself warm, I believe. Right, Ally?"

I give Mum and Andrea a tight smile and nod to close the topic then and there. It had been raining that morning when Dad briefly returned from the office for a change of clothes before leaving for another bunch of days. This mafia-busting case had been taking him to neighbouring cities all through the week. My surprised smiling self watched him jog towards me from the police jeep, unaware that this would be the last time I'd see him alive.

Two cups of yoghurt and a coffee later I follow Daze to the garage. He's humming something that sounds like "24K" by Bruno Mars and his upbeat mood makes me envious. I decide to shake off my dampened mood when he smiles at me while handing me the helmet.

Bro, hello? This cutie might like me, let's freaking go!

Less than 50 meters from St. Regis Ruler, I spot a blonde tall bun, secured with a pink rose and feel instant admiration for this eccentricity. I stare at her, watching as she eats cucumbers from a vendor, her familiar manicure giving her away.

On my request, Daze lets me off near the different snacks vendors that apparently line up by St. Regis every day. I wave at him and assure him I'll catch up; only then does he drive away. I walk over to the bespectacled lady and call out her name. She jumps, immediately pulls off her spectacles and imperiously turns towards me, her expression instantly changing to relief when she recognises me.

"Ally! Man, why you gotta scare a sis like that?" Daciana drawls, putting her spectacles back on.

"Daciana, you absolutely HAVE to teach me how to tie my hair like that."

"Mmm, I'd love to, Ally but I don't know how long it'll hold up because your hair is wayyyy longer than mine. By the way, cute butt!" She observes, peering at my back, while chomping on her cucumbers. I blush and take in her ruby-coloured shrug casually thrown over her black sports bra and slacks, so as to pass as decently dressed for college. Her tummy is solid, she really has a gorgeous bod and a face to walk the New York runway.

Before we start walking to college, Daciana promptly exchanges her spectacles for contact lenses and her slip-ons for a pair of slingback wedges. Her eyeliner still un-smudged, she looks like a celebrity with a midget-me trotting to keep up with her. She tells me about how she jogged all the way from her place to college because the weather was nice.

I don't run into any familiar faces when we make our way to Eco class. As we settle into our seats, Daciana solemnly says my name and pauses.

I look down at her face (because she's sitting and I'm standing, duh, otherwise there's no way my gnome-sized arse can look down on anyone). "Uhhh sorry for being cheesy Ally, but no one has ever given me this kind of importance that they left their other friends to come to me and even walk with me to college... Hell, people avoid meeting my eyes unless it's to check whether I've caught them STARING AT MY CLEAVAGE," she says this last part loudly enough for three of the leering classmates to look away, embarrassed, as they should be. "But you deliberately came to me... I... thanks Ally." She blinks and breaks eye contact with a small but genuine smile.

It makes me somewhat sad that people suffer for simply being themselves because of society's labels. Daciana is a simple, kind, and fun person. What is others' problem if she likes to feel comfortable in her own body? If she's confident; if she's real?

These fake Shikerdoodles will live a forced, plasticine, pathetic life and try to drown those too who attempt to break away. Never let them dictate how to live your own life. Do what makes you happy, but at the same time, don't hurt those who care for you while pursuing your happiness.

I wave off her thank-you speech, trying to explain that she seriously doesn't need to thank me for anything. I like her and that's why I choose to stick with her.

The session is interesting and I concentrate in the class. With about five minutes left before the next session, Daciana asks me what class I have next. When I tell her it's political science, she casually asks if I have someone from Daze's friend group in it with me. I shake my head no but tell her about FoxyJuhnson, and understanding dawns in her eyes.

She nods, "Yeah, even I don't know his name and frankly, I find him intimidating. He looks like he's always in the mood to drop kick someone. Weirdo."

This time I have a plan. I quickly bid a temporary farewell to Daciana and run to the next class. I quickly plant my arse on the same seat as yesterday, managing to avoid the awkward position. If FoxyJuhnson is late, he can easily decide whether to sit with me or not.

Hopefully, he won't, but a certain part of me is curious. Do not ask me why I pull a few strands out of my bun near my forehead so I don't look bald. Okay, he's entered—FUDGE. FUDGING.

NUGGETS!! HIS COLLARBONES ARE ON DISPLAY. RING THE FREAKING ALARMS.

Listen. He's wearing a navy shirt with the first two buttons unbuttoned. Listen. His grey jeans are folded as his puma sneakers are muddy. His matted blonde hair is wet and messy like he just got out of the shower but I know it's the rain. The sleeves of his shirt are rolled up, revealing a smartwatch on his toned forearms.

Are you listening?

Also, why the heck can't my vision work this clearly when I'm trying to see the whiteboard!? OKAY TIME TO STOP GOGGLING! ACT NATURAL, ALLY!

I rest my back against the chair and stretch my legs beneath the desk, trying to look chilled out, and start playing with my pencil pretending I'm lost in thought. It's comfortable for about three seconds before my dumb crocs start sliding on the floor and I begin to sink into my seat involuntarily. So, when a tall, lean foxy man halts beside me, I'm practically horizontal, with only my neck above the desk level.

Quite an appealing and relaxed look. Or not. He clears his throat—a nice rumbly growl. Mmmmm.

In an attempt to look at him as nonchalantly as possible, I turn my half-lidded eyes sideways, but given my awkward positioning, my eyes are in line with the zipper of his jeans. Yes, this is the second time my head is in front of his crotch and yet again, it's entirely involuntary. Gritting my teeth, I look up, realising I now resemble a cowering cattle, a sheep if you will. Fudge. His dark eyes hold a slight frown and his head tilts with…curiosity?

Either that or he can peer inside my tank top and is amused by my padded bra.

"Yes?" I manage to choke out meekly.

"Shift."

Ummm… am I supposed to say "Alt"? Are we naming keys? I'm still staring at him and his muggy hair flopping down on his forehead, when his eyes move to indicate the seat beside me. Oh, so he wants me to sit by the window? Nah, not in the rain.

"You can just round off the column from the front and occupy this. It's vacant."

Having said that and hoping he won't argue, I turn my head towards my pencil again. Okay, he still hasn't moved. OHHH SHIKERDO—he bends himself so that his face is at my eye level! He isn't quite in my personal space, but he's close and I can feel my face flushing.

"You're new here, aren't you, Pippi Longstockings? I think you need to know that I do not repeat myself; I don't take orders, I give them; and I do not like to hold conversations. So, shift."

HOLY SHIKERDOODLES, HOW DARE HE. Although he did not speak menacingly, he had a slight smirk. The cutest guy is always the a-hole. Kind of enraged, I sit up and stand to my fullest height before he can straighten. Hah! Now YOU talk to my uh… belly.

"You missed another thing that you don't do, you don't use your brain! INSTEAD of holding a conversation, you could've easily said, 'I'm lazy,' and I'd have moved. Huh, suit yourself." And just like that, I shift after having made my point.

His lower jaw juts out, and maybe he looks a little bit hot, but I refuse to acknowledge it because he's an egoist weirdo. He doesn't reply and I decide to ignore his existence which is ...hard because he falls in my line of sight when I try to look at the faculty.

Taking in EgoistFoxyJuhnson's broad shoulders and snug sleeves, the veins in his forearms popping, I try to ignore how his left leg drums a silent beat as his knee jiggles. He is not thickly built, but his shoulders are the broadest I've ever seen on a man. Broader than my dad's too, I think. Yeah, let's not think.

Wait. *Pippi Longstockings?* Who dat. I think she's a fictional character but I don't like the sound of her name. It reminds me of strawberry shortcake, which is what my ex used to call me (he called me Berry, don't ask). When the class is dismissed, I stand to leave but pause when I feel his eyes on me.

"I hope this new hairstyle saves you from further sacrifices..." he sneers.

HOW DARE HE. Enough. This shouldn't be used as leverage against me, especially when I'm still trying to build my identity here. I'll use HiN.

I lock eyes with him and concentrate on making him forget what happened. I repeat in my head: *You won't remember what happened between us yesterday.*

It usually takes about three to four seconds. His smirk fades. When I blink to conclude, he blinks too. Then he squints a little. Not wanting to get late for the next class, I don't wait for him to sort out his confusion and hurry to find Daze, comforted by the thought that at least he'll be with me in the next session. Daze is standing in the midst of the corridor, an enigma of male specimen.

When his eyes land on me, he smiles indulgently, and I can feel my cheeks flush as I smile in return.

"Ally." We start walking to the Psych class while his fingers gingerly reach for mine.

"You know, I want to be an architect."

"Oh? That's interesting, why is that?" Yep I've spoken my mind out loud, again.

"Hah, well first, I don't gotta leave home for work; second, money." He finishes with a flourish and I check to see when to laugh, but he doesn't look like he cracked a joke. Okay. It can't be that he hasn't researched the typical length of studies required to complete it.

Psych went on with the introduction of its branches. I was bored so I kept fiddling with my hair or my cardigan. Somewhere in between, I caught Daze's eyes and he was staring at me with a little smile. At times, I still find it too good to be true that someone as attractive as him could be so sweet AND affectionate towards me.

My next session is with Caecilia and I'm not sure whether she would want to sit with me, or rather, if I would want to sit with her. It's not that I owe her any apology or anything, Daze isn't an object that I snatched from her.

Daze drops me off at our seat and chats with Caecilia. It seemed to me like a light went off in her eyes when she saw us enter the room, shoulder to shoulder (though I made sure to skilfully extract my fingers from his before entering the room, with an excuse to straighten my cardigan). She seems gratified enough to be the centre of his attention, even when they're just discussing GoT again.

While leaving, Daze waves at her and blinks at me, and I can feel her noticing again. She continues fiddling with the zipper of her olive-green vest jacket, so I go ahead and greet her.

"How're you doing today, Caecilia?" I ask with a small smile.

She slowly looks at me like she's tired of some long conversation that we've had.

"Leave me alone, ALLY." Her voice drips with sarcasm and she's already gone back to tinkering with the zipper as if it's the most complicated of projects.

Before I can react, Mr Laabh arrives and I decide there's no point in making a big deal out of it. Besides, I was never too enthusiastic about conversing with Caecilia, especially when she's totally judgemental about women and can't see that if the guy she's been friends with since childhood hasn't cared for her yet, he won't start now.

FOUR

Considering how much I walked today; it seems reasonable to pick from today's biryani and selection of gravy for lunch. I know where to go. Daciana is at her usual junkies table, fiddling with her jackfruit gravy (ugh) and biryani. I pause and she catches my eye, so I beckon her. She shakes her head so I mock-frown and beckon her again, and she gives in.

Without a word, I walk with her toward Daze and the gang but I can feel her slowing down before we reach them. "Be yourself," I mutter as we halt in front of them.

"...because Jason Segel had that whole chain-smohking thing going on, thaht Lily girl didn't wanna kiss him aht all, man I'm telling you!" Fadil is booming excitedly while stuffing fried eggs into his mouth. Daze and Edie are listening but Caecilia is already looking at us, wide eyed.

"I wouldn't wanna kiss him even if he had a peppermint bush in his mouth." I comment and everyone's eyes swing to us. An "oh" slips out of an enraptured Fadil's mouth as his gaze takes in Daciana. A wary expression replaces Daze's smirk, but Edie still regards us coolly.

Everyone misses a beat before Daciana adds, "Smokers have no rights. It's not cool, it's not healthy, and your mouth smells like ass!"

Edie and I giggle, and even Daze cracks a smile. Fadil is now looking at all of us, surprised that we're all acting like nothing unusual has happened. All but Caecilia.

"What the hell is going on?" she bursts out.

She turns to me, "Who do you think you are, you barely fit in with that tomato ketchup mash on your head, and now you're bringing in Ms. Wonderbra?"

"Caecilia!" Daze interjects before I can reply.

Caecilia looks defiantly at Daciana. Daciana seems kind of unfazed and bears an expression which says she's embarrassed FOR Caecilia. Impressive. I have to learn this. My eyes catch her fingers shaking though.

"Caecilia, uhm, I think you should calm down…" Daze addresses her.

"And you should also apologize, dearie, to Daciana," I add, not caring much for her apology but needing to make sure this type of behaviour isn't normalised for Daciana.

Caecilia scoffs. Suddenly, Edie places her hand on Caecilia's shoulder. "This isn't cool, Caecilia," she says calmly and quietly.

Her eyes wary, Caecilia looks at all of us in turn. "Oh. You're ganging up on me," she mutters quietly.

Fadil takes a step towards her. "Aw man, c'mon naw, you're making a scene, Caecilia. Ohkay, you got beef with D, okay, sort iht out but don't create a telenovela right in front ohf my salad!"

My eyes meet Edie's and she gives me a blank stare, both of us stifling a smile. Silence pervades for a few seconds. Then, Daciana suddenly quips, "Um, so guys, I have news. Yesterday this new Italian café opened at Bano Garden Square which serves THE best Minestrone!"

She definitely had Fadil's attention with food and even Edie looked eager to hear what she had to say. From the corner of my eyes, I saw Caecilia's eye roll but she didn't interject further as Daciana described the setting of the café (ivy-covered walls and picnic tables).

Daciana has this habit of making gestures animatedly when she's excited and here she was, waving her hands about and bending her knees to exaggerate the height differences of various decor in the café. Anyone else would have looked goofy but it was her, so she just looked friendly and fun.

"I'm actually starting a shift there so I can get discounts for meals, but it's valid only till this weekend," Daciana paused.

"Wow, you have a job already? I have to be there! We have half-days on Saturdays, right?" I wondered aloud.

Daze looked sceptical, "I-uh, let's take one day to run it by ...our... parents and—" At my shocked expression, he backtracked. "—let's see if all of us are free this weekend because I have some errands at home and I'll need to check if I can get out of them," he finished with a small shrug. I looked at Edie who nodded, murmuring she'll probably be free, while Fadil avoided my eyes.

I knew what I had to do—intervene; but not in front of everyone, uh-huh. Flashing a smile at Daciana, I assured her that I'll be there and we'd see how this plan turns out. Daciana returned my smile but I could see it in her eyes; she knew rejection.

The boys resumed their conversation about some celebrity's personal life from E News! in front of an amicable listener Caecilia. Edie munched her spoonful solemnly, staring at nothing. This was not a great start but I will change things, I will.

I sidled up to Edie as it was now time to get back to our sociology lesson.

As soon as we reached the classroom, Edie dashed towards our seat. I hurried after her, anticipating someone hijacking our seat. Bruv, this really sucks. As if we don't have enough crap to deal with, now we're just trying to get a seat for, you know, actual education, and some rangy lad with a moustache has already dumped his stinky bag on our chair, so now you've got to do the walk of shame to the front row.

"Heyyy Edie, heyyy Ally! Wassup, ladies?" Gabby's earthy voice greets me. Edie stops in front of me but Gabby's built like the Burj Khalifa so I grin at her and compliment her on how her contrasting pink robes and green turban suit her.

I take my seat and ask Edie to sit as well. She looks mortified. Or maybe she's caught a chill in her bare arms. I bring it up. Gabby adds, "Hell naur, man, I don't even have a jacket but there's enough space in my robe for two, if you know what I mean, Edie!" We giggled while Edie turned bright red. Man, she's really shy.

The burgundy barbarian Mr Rachit was discussing group structures, norms, and conformities today. By the end of the lesson, I realise it isn't fair of me to push Edie out of her shell if she isn't comfortable at a particular moment.

Mr Rachit leaves us a few minutes before the bell. Edie is already looking expectantly towards Gabby and who could blame her? Gabby tells us that it was her younger brother's birthday yesterday, and he was out all evening so she had hidden beneath his bed to give him birthday bumps.

"And in walked that booger with a whole GIRL, and they freakin SAT on the bed... her arse was on my head! Their legs were poking each other like some freakin' chicken feet! That shxt was enough to put a girl off making out for life!"

We giggled but Edie's face went full haw, making Gabby widen her eyes before slipping into more giggles. As I headed for the next class, I realise Gabby was continuing her story—but only to the rapt attention of Edie. I pass by Fadil at the door who was calling her name but she didn't seem to hear him, because when I leave, they are still laughing.

History class was pretty empty when I walked in, but of course, he was there. FoxyJuhnson had taken his usual spot right by my seat, or rather, his, since it was on the adjacent column.

He's gawking at my desk, lost in thought but frowning. Thanks to my sneakers today, he doesn't sense me until I cease right in front of him. Maybe the HiN I exercised on him was too strong, what if he's become attached to me temporarily? Wouldn't that be too bad. With sympathy in my eyes, I look at him.

His frown stagnant, he exhales, "The last person who tried to *order* me, *fell* from the first floor *accidentally* and dislocated his shoulder. You are the second one to try."

Is he threatening me? And what even is he talking about?

"Are you still on about the seat shifting scene? Why are you so obsessed with a piece of furniture?"

"'*You won't remember what happened between us yesterday*' the hell was that?" he mimics.

Wait a minute.

A) I do not sound so squeaky.

B) He remembers what I said to him during HiN so that means that it didn't work.

C) He looks hot when he's angry. But why didn't it work? This is awkward.

"Eh, well do you?"

"Do I what?" he asks, resting his right arm on my desk and slightly leaning forward, so again I get distracted by the edge of his collarbones.

I close my eyes and inhale, "Do you remember what happened between us yesterday?"

"'Course I do, I chopped off your hair, Madam Pippi Longstockings, AND I had fun doing it."

He's smiling and pretending to look around my bun. Shikerdoodles. Do I try HiN again or... well, I'm hesitant. What if it fails again? I don't want to upset him over a small incident.

"Okay, first, my name is Ally. Second, I would highly respect it if you kept our business between us and keep the bro-code intact, know what I mean?" I wiggle my eyebrows in a manner I imagine to be attractive.

His smile doesn't fade, however, his frown has returned. "And why the hell would I follow the *bro-code* with you? I neither know who you are, nor do I want to." He straightens up with the last part.

Hey. That's mean. "Now, why would you not want to know me, is it my hair? Or is it because I'm too pretty, and you find me intimidating?"

Okay, now I'm simply provoking him. But who does he think he is, threatening me in the broad daylight? I have single-handedly put as many criminals behind bars as the number of years I have lived on this earth, I won't stand to listen to his male fudgenuggetry.

"Is it because you're—" he repeats my words and cracks up.

I place my books on my desk and hum nonchalantly as I wait for him to finish his pretend convulsion. "Hm."

He's still smiling, checking me out up and down now. Dear lord, what the heck? I can feel my cheeks getting warm.

"You aren't half bad but still not quite as intimidating as you think you are, Pippi."

HOW DARE HE.

I feel a sudden wave of impatience and take a step towards him. "Well, maybe you actually do not know me then, papi!"

His eyes widen, but he still looks amused. Okay fudge, I did not just call him daddy in Spanish. His lips part and I catch a glimpse of how his left incisor is a tiny bit chipped at the corner. Suddenly, Fadil's 'hey' breaks through the air and Foxyjuhnson's smile leaves his face. He rolls his eyes instead and slumps into his seat.

My butt suddenly heavy, I plant myself in my chair too—but not before exchanging a glance with FoxyJuhnson. "You're buddies with him now or what?" Fadil is breathing beside me. I dismiss his query with a shake of my head.

I try hard to concentrate on the lesson, and after what seems like an eternity, the bell goes off. I hurriedly gather my stuff and almost make a run for it, but curiosity makes me pause. When I turn my head, my eyes land squarely on his, which are also boring into mine.

This time, his eyes have no emotion, just depth. We don't exchange any silent messages, or meaningful context, but merely hold each other's gazes. I am the first to break the moment, turning away, and passively continue walking.

Daciana joins me on the stairwell. She's let her hair down for Anthro, and we know it's because of that cute geek she's got her eyes on. I don't understand what's stopping him from asking her out; she looks like a bombshell in the simplest of outfits, and that is because of her amazing personality.

Ms Olivia is not backing down with her usual threatening tone, "I want a refresh of the last class. How many branches are we studying this sem?"

"That would be social and cultural, ma'am." I don't need to turn my head to know the confident, disembodied voice belongs to the hot geek Daciana has a crush on.

"Not quite right, are we, Heath?"

A silence falls over the classroom in the face of an expectant Ms Olivia. "I'm surprised even you don't know it, Heath. Whoever gets it right would not only earn my appreciation but yours too," she announces controversially.

"Archaeology and linguistics, go!" I urgently murmur into Daciana's ears and lift her arm so it shoots up in response. Daciana twists her head around in alarm as if someone just shouted, '*Is that Selena Gomez?*'

"Daciana? You have something on your mind?" Ms Olivia seems genuinely confused.

"Uh, I ..." Daciana stammers, then finally notices my furious scribbling. "The other two branches are linguistics and archaeology?" Ms Olivia pauses. She places her diary down on the table and smiles.

"Heath, I believe you owe Daciana a pat on the back." Ms Olivia's words were followed by multiple sniggers and suggestive throat clearings from the back benches. Daciana turned the colour of her lips. A few awkward seconds later, Heath's hand tapped Daciana's shoulder lightly, and he said, "Well done." Oh! For once, he didn't sound as snotty as his usual expression suggested he was.

To get Daciana to respond, I had to positively poke her in the thigh. It was only then that she composed herself and turned her head to flash a genuine smile at Heath, mumbling a small 'thank you.'

The rest of the lesson went by amusingly as every few minutes Daciana had the realisation that her crush had 'fingered her shoulder,' as she put it, and widened her eyes in thin air. Apparently, they exchanged glances at the end of the class too, judging by the way she squeezed my palm as he passed by. Needless to say I was in a good mood when I spotted Daze traipsing towards our commerce class with Fadil and a bunch of other guys.

Daze and the guys were joking around, and the corridor they were in intersected with the hallway where I was standing near an opening by the stairs. In a flash, I watched in horror as Daze walked into none other than FoxyJuhnson! FoxyJuhnson slowly twisted sideways on his ruddy Pumas, facing Daze.

I didn't wanna be the recipient of the screwed-eyed, un-amused, sinister smile he threw at Daze as he uttered in a husky voice, "Get into this bumpy-chumpy binness only with your mates, yeah Keberkil?" I don't know what came over Daze, but he took off his sunglasses to glare at FoxyJuhnson!

His eyes met mine for a second and he put his glasses back on with a grin, but not before responding, "You first, three chins."

???????? Huh?? Okay, first of all, that was completely uncalled for, considering it was Daze who collided into FoxyJuhnson; and secondly, he DEFINITELY doesn't have three chins. He has a beautiful sharp jawline and a robust Adam's apple and his—um. Where was I? YEAH, so fat-shaming? That is a complete no-no. I made a mental note to tackle Daze later about it.

Now, let me describe the view that I was beholding. Daze, looking way too pleased with himself, marched towards me while behind him, FoxyJuhnson strode, still fuming over the unnecessary verbal attack at his appearance. He gritted his teeth, and gradually extended his arm to grab Daze's right shoulder, and I imagine, rightfully punch him. Not too late, I recall the buttock dagger he has. OHMYGOD FOXYJUHNSON IS GOING TO KILL MY CRUSH!!

Not on my watch.

I collect my thoughts and stare intensely into FoxyJuhnson's dark eyes. HiN is working in overdrive, though I don't think it's effective from a distance, but there's no harm in trying. His eyes suddenly do lock with mine and I will him to calm down and drop this. *Calm down baby, calm down and breathe.* He pauses for just a second, still frowning, the anger in his deep eyes giving way to confusion, and then, deflation. He drops his arm. Wow. It worked. Even with the headache.

"Ally, you're a sight to behold after the world's most boring lecture!" Daze announces and I feel my cheeks blushing immediately.

Instead of this hot guy flirting, my gaze followed FoxyJuhnson's disgusted blinks and his final top-to-bottom assessment of me, which he clearly doesn't like, judging by his heavy exhale as he enters the classroom.

Mrs Aubrey dives headfirst into accountancy today, and while Daze is passing notes and staring into space, I find myself really interested in the lecture for once. Mum says that with my *gift*, I'm meant to join police intelligence. I haven't given it much thought, but the idea gives me bittersweet vibes.

When the final bell is about to ring, I'm almost sad that the lecture is over. As an excuse to steer me through the crowd, Daze casually holds my upper arm. I appreciate the gesture, even though I know where the exit is.

While we wait in the shed, Daze starts humming a song and nodding his head. I'm unable to recognise it, so he finally tells me it's some Barbara Streisand song, and he just can't resist the urge to dance to it. How prince Charles of him.

Soon, the gang walks in, and predictably, Caecilia brightens at the tune of that weird Barbara Streisand number. She starts shimmying in front of Daze who goofily returns the move. So, there are two people shaking their boobs at each other, while my gaze darts from one pair of boobs to another. Um.

I try to shake off this image from my head as Daze and I ride off into the sunset... I mean, with the sun over our heads towards BurgerOns. Apparently, on Tuesdays and Thursdays, they serve grilled prawns too. The whole group digs into them, while the vegetarians—Edie and I—chew on our burgers. Isn't it a little insensitive that Daze, fully knowing that I detest eating animals, sits right in front of me and downs one sea creature after another?

Not being one of those veganism lawyers, I refrain from inquiring Daze about it, but somewhere inside, I'm hoping for an apology or an acknowledgement at the least. Subconsciously, I don't even lean towards him on the scooty on our way to the barn. I don't think he notices, though.

Bracing myself for the poo smell to hit, I follow the gang inside. But—wonders! It's the scent of some antibacterial liquid instead. Just as bad. The shed compartments are being cleaned.

All the horses are tied to edges of the windows, with a spare nail here and there jutting out from the walls of the Blabamas' residence. Fadil, Edie, and Caecilia make their way to their buddy horses while I falter. Of course, I won't look a gift horse in the mouth (is that how this stupid idiom is used?) and follow Daze like a distressed damsel in a tank top.

Moreover, I hadn't exactly considered how my boobs would bounce on the horse and the balcony view that Daze would have down my chest, seated behind me.

Apprehension clouded my mind as I strolled around the barn. At one moment, I got this feeling like my movements were being watched. Expecting a certain male gaze, I smiled and turned, only to find myself square frontal with a chocolate-coloured, silky-coated cutie who was clearly regarding me with keen interest.

Now, I don't know what goes on in a four-legged creature's mind, but he definitely seemed like he was smirking. Unable to restrain myself, I walked up to him and gently caressed his snout. He leaned into my palm.

That was it. I was in love. I stared deeply into his eyes and we were having a moment (no I wasn't HiN-ing him), until Daze's voice interrupted, "I wish she'd look at me like that, Olive."

"You'd have to be as tall, dark, and handsome as him then," I replied. "Does he go by the name Olive?"

"Yeah, and he's usually not very active. Maybe you turn him on... I mean towards activity."

Uh-huh, boys seem to be out of my league, but maybe I could *whin* with horsies? Never mind.

"Can you teach me how to put a saddle on, Daze?" I smiled at him.

His blush was almost immediate, followed by a sprint to the barn. Softly, I bent towards Olive's nose and gently touched it with mine. It was really calming.

"Can we take him home?" I moaned to Daze as he showed me where the saddle belt went around Olive's stomach and how to fasten his reins.

"If you're this sweet to his actual owner, mogul guy, maybe he will let you take just this one."

As Daze steered Olive towards the field, I built up the courage to decline his offer to help me ride. "I was wondering if I could spend some time alone with Olive and get to know him better..."

Daze looked taken aback. "For real? You'll be able to handle him?"

"I would really like to try."

He thought it over for a few seconds before nodding, "Alright then, just remember how to shepherd him right and left and halt him. Don't make him gallop. Be back here by 4."

"Aye, aye, cap'n!" I have to admit he looked cute giving instructions.

Olive and I set off before the others could. I had no specific direction in mind so I just let Olive take the lead. The green field seemed to stretch on endlessly, the horizon barely visible. The wind was cool and Olive's pace was steady and comfortable.

The last time I had felt this relaxed was when my dad had tried to disentangle my hair as a child. He was always so careful not to pull at them and loosened the locks with deliberate, gentle movements, taking his own sweet time. It made me feel sleepy.

Hmm. How long had I been lost in my own thoughts? Which direction is the barn again? Why can I not spot any sign of human civilisation? I urge Olive to move a bit faster, but even after four or five minutes, I am unable to guess where we are. Shikerdoodles. Am I lost? I'll just call Daze. This isn't a movie so don't worry; my phone is charged and I do have network coverage. Tee-hee.

"Yeah Ally, what's up?"

"Daze? I...think I am a bit off the track."

"Um... can you see any landmarks?"

“Not really, just some tripod-shaped bushes scattered here and there… Isn’t there some rule that if I walk in a specific direction, I’ll eventually reach somewhere? But I’m not sure which direction to go to have the best chance of getting back on time.”

“Let me check… the barn is towards the North, I think. You stick to the North direction and call me if you find anything unusual and identifiable, okay?”

Easy. I turn on the compass on my smartphone and head north. It’s hard to be tense when I have such a great pal as Olive with me. I hum a little tune. A song. Two songs. Has it been fifteen minutes already? There’s something on the horizon at the northeast... maybe the battlements of a castle-like ruin. WHAT on earth is a historic building doing in the middle of private land? Wait—it’s not a ruin. It’s quite solid and upright.

What if it’s haunted or something? Ha! Now I must check it out. I coax Olive towards the manmade structure and he obediently complies. The building is somewhere between a mansion and a castle, built of stone with an ominous design. It has a functional lived-in look.

The outer boundary has a giant rusty gate that’s slightly ajar. The yard is overgrown with wild bushes, but I can spot heavy wooden doors, now that I’m closer. The doors don’t match the stone exterior’s ancient, dated look. Maybe it’s someone’s holiday home? It might still be haunted, there’s hope alright.

I’ve reached close enough now to walk in.

I tie Olive’s reins to the grill door so he can make a noise and alert me if he wants to run. Tentatively, I step onto the premises and run my eyes around the yard. There are no dead leaves or twigs on the pebbled footpath leading to the door, so there must be a caretaker present to keep it clean.

They are not doing a good job though, because the creepy gargoyles on the posts are dusty as heck. I can't spot a bell or metal knocker on the door, and it seems too heavy to just tap with my knuckles to make a sound.

Now I have two options:

1. A) Slap on the door like a forlorn cowboy and shout, "Heyyyyooo!"
2. B) Back away and sprint a bit before slamming shoulder-first onto the door.

As graceful as both the options seem, I end up doing a combination of both. My shoulder meets the door (no sprinting, though) and I call out, "Is someone in?"

Once. Twice.

On my third shoulder-slam-knock attempt, I sense the door move. A middle-aged lady with sharp features in a proper maid's uniform opens the door.

"Hello? Sorry to disturb you, but what is this place? Do you live here?"

I keep my tone polite and concentrate on maintaining a friendly expression. I hear another female voice ask the maid something as she approaches. With her Selena Gomez resemblance (but skinnier), her curious gaze shifts to one of confusion as she frowns at me.

She's pretty, maybe a little younger, and looks like she has just seen me sprout a beard out of nowhere. To my chagrin, I don't think I'd look bad with one.

"Uhhh hi, how'd you get here?" she asks, eyeing me up and down. I can't help but wish my long hair were as calm and demure as hers, resting neatly on either side of her torso.

"Hello, I seem to have lost my way. You see, I was out with Olive, and Daze told me to go North but there were bushes and my phone still had a signal, you know..." I trailed off as she tilted her head much like a confused puppy listening to human speech.

"How may I help you?" she diffidently asks.

"Can you tell me the way to the Blabamas' barn?"

"Do you work there?" She checked me out again.

"No," I peered inside. The floors were white marble. There was no foyer, just one large hall with a fireplace and an entire wall of French doors with the curtains drawn back.

"We were just visiting him. It's my first time here."

She seems thoughtful for two seconds and exchanges a few quiet words with the maid, whose expression remains neutral, before she smiles slightly and opens the door wider. "Okay, I'll have my brother drop you off when he comes. Come on in."

Gratefully, I stepped into the regal living room, consisting of a fur-laced navy blue sofa set, glass chandeliers, and minimalist decor. "Sorry for being nosy again, but do you live here full time?"

"Please have a seat."

"Um, may I ask where the restroom is?"

"It's towards the left, the first white door you spot," the maid replies.

The hall was huge, it took me a long while to reach the sofa. Skinny Selena walked past me and stepped through one of the French doors. "Excuse me, I have to get back to my acroyoga session," she said cheerfully before disappearing.

Acrowhat? Anyway, the interiors looked finer than the exteriors. Not going to lie, I'm kind of looking forward to checking out the restroom.

The hall opens into a narrow passage that leads to a circular plaza-like space, where a pristine white staircase ascended beyond my sight. Anyway, the restroom must be behind this white door. The wallpapers here are interesting—kinda Mexican-inspired patterns in warm orange and gold undertones. The modern decor had me imagining a typical mall-like washroom, but weirdly enough it was a cosy, single-occupancy bathroom with a bathtub, toilet, and sink with a mirror.

It was unnervingly quiet for a mansion of this size. Back in the hall, I walked up to the French doors and admired the view of what was supposed to be the backyard. Backyard? People have trampolines and inflatable tubs in their backyard. Skinny Selena had a whole pool, a fountain, and an acrobatics pole in hers. Beyond it stretched a garden.

Daze's call broke my envious reverie. I answered immediately. "Hiii, listen, I found a big arse palace in the middle of nowhere here and they seem helpful enough—"

"PEOPLE?! You found people there?"

"Well, Yeah," I replied. It seemed he'd be less incredulous if I'd reported aliens instead.

"There's this girl and she has a brother who'll probably drop me off. I know it's getting late, so the others can go home, but can YOU stay?"

"Of course, Ally. Keep me updated, okay?"

"Sure. Thanks, Daze." He's really sweet. Not even once did he get annoyed with me for wanting to explore alone even when I kinda messed up.

A male voice in the distance shouted, "Leave it! Let it go!" I looked up to find Skinny Selena and a very gorgeous guy hanging onto the acrobatics pole with their clenched thighs!

They were forming some kind of an outstretched star-like stance but Skinny Sel simply looked like she was struggling to hold in number two. Unsure of what to do, I awkwardly started clapping which caused the duo to stop whatever they were doing and drop down immediately. I make people fall off poles. Wonder how that'll look on my resumé. Mortified, I made my way back to the sofa. If I sit primly enough, maybe it'll be like that never happened.

"Hey, are you hungry or something? We're going to have some gram salad," Skinny casually asked as they walked in.

"No, thank you, I just had my lunch from BurgerOns—you know, the one that's like two blocks away?"

She looked thoughtful. "Is the food there even sanitary enough?"

Huh? "I guess so."

"Oh, okay." She smiled a small smile and proceeded down the hall.

It was twenty minutes to four already. Daze and the gang would usually start leaving for home in a few minutes. I wonder when Skinny's brother would be here and drop me back.

Where are all the adults in this house? Why is it so quiet in here? No sounds of the maid from any kitchen or anyone walking around. Why does the inside of the mansion not have a lived-in feel? I've been here for half an hour and into four living spaces already, but I have yet to spot a personal item (unless you count the acrobatics pole).

Where is the staff who must be responsible for keeping such a huge building pristine? WHY is it so isolated? How does Skinny go to school? Why was her yoga teacher clasping hands with her? And so on. I will definitely pester the Blabamas about this later.

A slight scuffle breaks my contemplation of these very meaningful universal questions. There's a figure at the door. A male figure. Oh thank lord, maybe the brother is finally here. The man walks confidently from the dark shadows near the door towards the hall… towards me.

Okay, should I stand up or will that seem too meek? Cos he's definitely not an elder. Should I wave?

He seems to slow down, no wonder because he can see a stranger sitting with her butt on his clean rich sofa set.

But what if he's someone else and not the brother? My eyes flick to the corridor on the other side, silently pleading Skinny Selena to appear, though it's unlikely that she could have finished her salad in ten minutes. The guy walks to the middle of the hall and pauses. His handsome face contorts into a mix of confusion and distaste.

"Unbelievable," he breathes, but his voice echoes so I hear him clearly. I stand up indignantly and glare right back at FoxyJuhnson.

FIVE

"YOU!?" I exclaim at the same time he says, "Why the hell are you following me?!"

Seeing me blink rapidly, he continues, "HERE!? LITERALLY no one knows where I live. Literally!"

Abruptly, he darts forward and stops just one step away from me, near the sofa.

"You a spy or something?" he whispers conspiratorially.

That's enough. Raising my hands in a defensive position, I try to calm him, "Listen. I am JUST NOW finding out that YOU own this place, and that too because you blurted it out RIGHT NOW."

He frowns, but it's less of a frown and more of a hurricane forming right in the middle of his eyes. "WHAT EVEN are you doing here!? LITERALLY HOW."

An automatic nodding spree makes its way out of me as a way of explanation. Yes, cool af.

Not.

"I lost my way. I was with Olive, you see..."

His head starts flailing about as if he's expecting the horse to come trotting about and ruin his precious marble floors any minute now.

"And Olive is...??"

"He's a horse I borrowed from the Blabamas... they live on the outskirts of these fields?" Realisation thankfully dawns on his face. We skipped a beat.

"You… cannot find your way back?"

"Yes." Another beat.

"Why are you alone? Where is that salt-and-pepper-haired jock strap of a guy who holds your reins?"

Disloyally, I burst out a giggle at his description but managed to make it sound challenging with regard to the latter half of his statement.

"A) No GUY can hold my reins; and

B) I'm quite capable of riding a horse on my own; and

C) Particularly, I have zero interest in standing here and answering your trivia quiz, so if you'd be kind enough to point me in the right direction, I'll get going."

My legs carry me past him as I finish my impassioned speech. With some glee, I notice his head turn and follow me. Tee hee.

"You're planning to go back on that horse?"

"Certainly, Ms Lisa Simpson, or would you suggest swimming all the way across the greens?"

The hurricane on his forehead is back. "Woah, woah, woah. Pippi Longstockings said what?"

What was that quote of hers from the book? Something about giving children love, more love, and common sense will come to them? Yeah.

"She asked me to give you love, and maybe common sense will follow?"

I kept walking towards the door and didn't look back. No way am I going to ask for any help from this guy. A few seconds later, I am about to open the door but I feel his presence right behind me.

Usually, I have this instinct to hit anyone who comes this close to my space all too sudden because that person's intention is never good. This is what my father taught me. All I had to do now was jerk my head back so it hits his neck or jaw, and headbutt into his gut while he's still dazed.

Surprisingly, FoxyJuhnson's body heat crackling against mine did not have a sinister feel. Even more surprisingly, I felt myself relax. Neither of us spoke nor moved for a few seconds. My back inches from his chest, my eyes fixed on the door knob.

Then his voice, nothing but a husky bass, broke the silence. "Wait a minute. You still won't be able to find your way back with your horse. Don't make rash decisions out of anger."

It sounded like the fight had abruptly left his system. The change in his tone was so startling that I was left dumbstruck. Turning around tardily, I tried to meet his eyes to comprehend what had caused this change. He only looked into mine for a second before looking downward (not at my boobs).

"It's getting late, I should have been back like fifteen minutes ago. I've got to get going somehow."

"I'll drop you."

"I don't want to bother you like that. If you could just make me a map or like, point out some landmarks, I'll find my way back myself."

"Landmarks on a grass field? What, like take a right where the grass is slightly greener?" His voice was returning to its usual tone, and so was his mood. I looked at him deadpan. He was frowning, but by gosh, he was gorgeous.

Decisively, he took a step towards the door and opened it, then paused on the threshold and looked back at me.

"Come on now."

He kept moving. In this unknown place, I definitely was at his mercy, but not quite helpless, mind you. I stretched my neck in case a quick headbutt was required. By the time I started following him, he was halfway down on the forlorn garden porch area, towards the right side of the mansion. Parked there were a big blue and silver SUV, a golden scooter and a red Apache motorcycle. And sure enough, FoxyJuhnson had his butt planted on it.

Now, I am against the idea of running Olive at the speed of a motorcycle and exhausting him. FoxyJuhnson will just have to drive at a strolling pace with his RACER bike. But how will I convey this to him? Sigh.

"Ain't doing anything like that."

FoxyJuhnson shook his head and half-smiled. Shikerdoodles. I've spoken aloud again. He's pulled up next to me. Waiting. Blank is what I am.

"Please put one and one together quicker, Pippi. You are lively in the morning."

"What about Olive?" I ask as darkly as I can.

"Your best friend Olive will be taken back to his owner. Now get your bum back there, I literally have other things to do."

Man, he is irritated more than necessary. Can't a girl be concerned about non-humans? Jeez. Moving on, I cannot believe the humiliation—hitching a ride from the enemy? This is more embarrassing than when I mistook a guy wearing fashionable sunglasses for a blind man and tried to forcibly pull him across a road he clearly didn't want to cross.

Frowning (so he knows I am not enjoying this at all), I hopped onto the motorcycle and found that my chest was level with his shoulders. Have you seen how Apaches are built? The back seat slants up at about forty-five degrees. One break and I'll be slamming boobs-first into his head. Hmm. Just gonna hold the back of the seat.

Okay, this isn't working. As soon as he accelerated, my arse slid forward and now my thighs are touching his. But I had to pick between my boobs or thighs, so…

It felt like my back might give out any moment from the way I was twisting and stretching to avoid smashing into him. Even if I do, his head seems quite fluffy. Unruly dirty blond locks, a bit on the longer side. Sadly his neck isn't visible. Don't ask why it's sad.

He's driving quite fast since the land isn't bumpy, and the forty-five-degree slant of the seat really serves its purpose. Hate to admit it, but the ride is not half bad, especially now that I'd discovered that FoxyJuhnson's hair smells like salt and beaches.

"Your jock pals are going to be there to drive you home, right?"

"Yeah, you know the Blabamas, don't you?"

I subconsciously lean forward, bringing our faces closer than comfortable. His face turned towards me, and his sidelocks brushed against my cheek.

"Not exactly. Look, I'll take you to the edge of this landscape, then you can walk the perimeter until you reach that thick-necked guy."

A laugh escaped my lips. "You should just sue his parents at this rate for birthing him."

"But then I'd have to see his constipated face every week in court."

He had a half smile playing on his lips. I blinked in surprise, realising it's the first time I've seen him genuinely smile.

"He is not constipate—um."

We share a laugh—wait, what? Am I actually joking around with the enemy? Regrettably (!?), the road and signs of human life started coming to sight. In order to dismount, I lightly touched his shoulder to balance myself. Very normal of me to mention every single point of contact with a guy like I'm a Mormon.

"Hello Daze? I'm back to civilisation and I'm near the pottery shop at the end of the field. Does that ring a bell?"

"Thank gosh, yeah, I know which one, Ally. We'll be there in a few minutes."

He sounds pretty relieved. FoxyJuhnson has already turned his bike around to leave. Nodding once accompanied by a bready smile (you know, the kind where your lips stretch into dimples but you're not actually smiling—yeah, like a loaf of bread), I mutter a quick thanks. He raises an eyebrow. Hate to admit it but I still can't help feeling he's a jerk. Why is he SO RUDE.

He starts his motorcycle and retraces his path. It takes about seven minutes for Daze, Fadil, and everyone else to reach me. Edie and Daze come jogging as soon as they get off their vehicles. Eeeee, Daze looks so worried, there are beads of sweat on his forehead. It looks as if he might embrace me (a most welcome act), but he stops short very close to me.

"Ally."

"Daze."

Instinctively, my palm finds his and we squeeze each other.

"Daze looked ready to throw up in your absence, Ally," Edie blurts out.

"It's also the same face which he mahkes when Caecilia plucks his monobrow—OW! Whatcha doh that for!?" Fadil rubs his chest where Daze slapped him, looking pained.

We start to leave but not before Caecilia accuses me of losing Olive. "I found a helpful family and they know the Blabamas. They'll make sure Olive reaches home alright."

Do not ask me why I didn't disclose it was FoxyJuhnson's family.

A warm shower at home hit all the right spots. But somehow, the migraine was returning. After changing into a cozy pink cardigan and slacks, I wondered what I could find in the kitchen for my rumbling stomach.

"Ally? Open the door."

It was Daze, holding a tray with two sundae cups. Manually customised with cashews and chocolate sauce. Can there BE a better boyfrien—uh, BOY?

"I had a feeling you'd be in the mood for some ice cream after SUCH an upsetting adventure."

"Mmph, if playing along with your damsel-in-distress plot gets me fudge ice cream, then I'll go off wandering the moors every day." I replied, sucking on the cool vanilla cream.

We sat perched on my bed as dusk settled in. The only light in the room came from the fading daylight filtering through the window, which casted a soft glow over the purple flower garden outside. Daze's neck looked exquisite in his washed-out black shirt. It didn't help that he kept giving me long sideways glances with the spoon between his glistening lips.

"Hopefully you won't think it was pansy of me, but I really was all out of breath and distressed when you hadn't returned for an hour. I was running about like a… fool," he chuckled sadly.

"I regret that you went through so much trouble because of me…" I couldn't look him in the eyes.

He leaned towards me. "Heyy," he said softly. "It's okay."

Shyly lifting my head, I found him at the perfect distance for a lip lock. Instead, I blurted out, "It's unbelievable how beautiful your eyes are."

Girls, sometimes being honest is very rewarding, which I'll demonstrate further with this moment. My words made him sigh like he was controlling an urge to smush his face into mine. The next thing I knew, his fingers gently caressed my jaw before turning my face towards him.

This was it. I was getting kissed by the cutest guy I'd ever met. Hopefully, there's no pistachio crumb on my lip. Is it okay to start chewing your lover's stray pista piece if it gets in the way of your nom-noming?

"What I feel for you Ally, is part an urge to protect you, part an urge to kiss your lips, part an urge to go surfing with you and part an urge to keep my head on your chest and hear your heartbeat."

Shikerdoodles! The last part though? Does he doubt my vitality or is it an excuse to feel my breasts?

"And which urge is the loudest, Daze?" I asked, barely a whisper.

His hand cups my face in response and he pauses. I close my eyes, waiting for the moment, but instead it's his thumb which softly grazes my lips. Um, how long should I keep my eyes closed? Will he kiss me right now or what? Maybe I do have pista crumbs on my lips and he is just brushing them off. Then it happened, his lips did a *chu* on my forehead. Huh, guess his guardian instinct prevailed. Fudge pistachios, man.

Smiling, we both knew that the moment had come to an end. We went back to our sundaes, but not before I squeezed his palm. My migraine was too persistent for me to analyse what Daze's actions implied. Maybe I'll discuss it with Daciana tomorrow.

"Tomorrow morning?" Daze smiled at me before leaving my room.

"See you then." I hope my blush wasn't too evident.

Ugh, homework. Let's get on with it. The painkiller only managed to dull my headache. If it doesn't subside by tomorrow, I'm going to see a doctor.

I couldn't sleep properly at all. My nightmare consisted of endlessly running through those purple flowers and hearing the roar of a motorcycle engine, but seeing nothing. Needless to say, my goal for today was to finish school as soon as possible and let my head hit the pillow on priority.

Clothes? Just going to throw on this green sweater vest on my dark camisole and trousers, so it's not too sexy for school. Hair down, yellow knit ballet flats, kohl, BB cream, and lipstick—can we be done already?

When the whiff of fried onions hit me from the breakfast table, I was done getting ready. Daze was happily chomping away and paused just enough to greet me with a sincere smile, which I doubt I returned. Pouring myself some coffee I started blowing on it to cool it down.

"Why Aaliah, you forgot your T-shirt under your sweater?" Sigh.

"Um, Mrs Keberkil, do we have cornflakes?"

"Why would you want cornflakes when I've fried onion pakodis especially for breakfast?"

"That's sweet of you Mrs Keberkil, but I don't feel up for it this early."

Mrs Keberkil muttered something about "this generation's girls" and their "foolish dieting habits" as she went off to fetch me a box of cornflakes. I decided I was not in the mood to argue this early in the morning.

"St. Regis being too hard on you, Ally?" Daze took a bite out of his pakodi, still smiling. How are people morning persons? Make it make sense.

"Not really, I just couldn't sleep too well."

Daze cupped his hand near his mouth and whispered, "Try my bed today!" We both giggle.

Resting my cheek against Daze's shoulder, clad in a vintage T-shirt, my migraine started to ease on the way. Maybe it was the breeze, maybe it was him; I didn't have anything to complain about. A downside to this was that I was already sleepy by the time we reached St. Regis.

We were greeted at the shed by the gang, where Caecilia gave me the once-over and then whispered something not too complacently to Edie. Before I could prepare a reply for the forthcoming snide remarks, a blur in cream faux fur buried my face in something soft which smelled faintly of expensive wood.

"Daciana!" I greeted Daciana's breasts. Not to be lezzy, but this was not a bad feeling at all.

"Ally, babe! Come with me quick, I have something for you..." she said, gently pulling me away right after I waved hello to Fadil and Edie, and handed me a chewy toffee.

"You didn't just have this candy to dish out after you called me that urgently, Daciana, so spill!"

"Okay, so I bumped into Heath at Ava bakery yesterday afternoon…" Her eyes twinkled and she looked charming with her hair in a loose bun.

"Ooooh when? After school?"

"Uh-huh, I was there buying a mango shake and bumped right into his back butt-first. He turned around and his 'sorry' got caught midway in his throat and he froze RIGHT IN MY FACE with his cheesy burger halfway to his mouth! We stood like that for two silent seconds until he swallowed what he was chewing and said 'hey.'"

We widened our eyes at each other as we entered the classroom. Her voice lowers a pitch. "Then he said, 'Hey, you've been studying these days?' and I nodded because ya know, I didn't trust myself not to blurt out 'yeah I've straightened my horns' or something."

"Then we had like this… nodding competition where he nodded for some reason and I nodded because he did and we bobble-headed for a minute until he broke this head beatboxing with a 'Yep. Great. See you in class then!' and exited."

"Oooooh I take that as the first base of your relationship?"

"Shut up Ally, oh shit, he's in... SHHHH!"

We watched as the apple of her eyes—at the moment, it's Heath—walked in, clutching his thick textbook. "Today, you'll catch him at the end of this period and ask him a doubt. But you need to know the context of that doubt so you can catch him off-guard with your geniosity again."

"Okay redhead cupid, if this goes well, I'm asking you out on a date first!"

"I'll hold you to that!"

The lesson on elasticity of demand went by interestingly. Not so much for Daciana, though who—despite having a motivation with a hair gel and glasses—was doodling on the diagram, designing the flag for some Middle Eastern country.

As the teacher gathered up his books to leave, I nudged Daciana. "See Daciana, ask him what might be some examples of perfectly inelastic demand. If he can't come up with anything, suggest—listen carefully—'vegetables? Because they might sell at any price due to their perishability?'"

We went over the question twice before Daciana felt confident enough to approach Heath. Heath's friends were ogling at her but she paid them no heed. Watching her lean towards him while consulting her (mine) notebook makes me realise she can actually pull it off. And hey, I don't have the migraine anymore. Phew.

Woah, Heath just widened his eyes at something she said. Not in a bad way, but a good one, like 'Hey Stephen Hawkings just won the election for POTUS' kinda widen.

By the time I nonchalantly walk towards them to pick her up, he's surrendered two smiles and an eyebrow raise. "Well?"

"Ally, you're such a lifesaver, if I don't end up with Mr Gorgy glasses, I'll marry you!"

I'm still imagining that it's not a half-bad prospect when I'm reminded of a full bad prospect who happens to be sitting next to me in political science. The prospect, donned in a Hawaiian shirt and black jogger ninja pants, regards me in what I would shamelessly pronounce as a lecherous manner.

My hair is the colour of fresh lava, which earns me frequent stares. Like any other woman, the gaze of men is all too familiar to me. But not all gazes make me flush like his does. His eyes intimidate me as they court me to the seat. At last, I meet his glare head-on. About two seconds later, he breaks off our staring contest with a secret smile to himself. Hmph. Let him keep his joke to himself, I'm definitely not going to be the one to speak first.

"Can you fudge your nuggets off?"

I cannot believe *these* are the words that arranged themselves in a sequence and chose to leave my mouth at such a crucial moment.

He bursts into a snigger. "My nuggets? You want me to make a fudge out of my nuggets?"

Keep your lashes low, Ally. You're on the verge of giggling yourself.

"Please share the recipe, Pippy, I'm enthralled as to how to proceed." He's silently laughing, and looking pretty attractive. Darn it.

Public policy and administration isn't half as attractive as FoxyJuhnson smiling to himself every few minutes and darting looks at me. If this isn't flirting, I don't know what is.

On his fifth smirk, I lean a bit towards him and say, "You're in a good mood today." He immediately whips his head and holds my gaze. His eyes are dark and appealing.

"You are the only non-relative person I've had at my place. This doesn't just happen. How did you manage to make your way there? This refuses to make sense to me."

"I guess Olive finds you irresistible."

He rolls his eyes at my innocent blinking. "Well, I should anticipate the jock strap and the thick broccoli-necked-brothers finding me irresistible pretty soon too, huh?"

BROCCOLI! Poor Fadil! "They are straight, and even if they weren't, I doubt you'll be a boy magnet. Also, WHY are we talking about your possible dates?"

"Man, I dunno either! Just... you must have told them everything, right?" He doesn't sound very pleasant now.

"About?"

"About us!"

"About US!?"

"Why is my voice echoing?" He raises a single eyebrow at me.

"What *about* us?"

He frowns silently at my counter-question, though his expression lacks temper. His eyes seem lighter than usual and I can't even see my reflection in them. His jawline is so sharp one could sharpen knives on them. Call me superficial, but I don't want to keep arguing with someone so gorgeous. Zaekhuru ON. Focus. I try to mould his soul with my gaze.

His frown gradually recedes as I softly say, "Don't quarrel with me."

Two beats pass. Seems like I have succeeded in getting my message across with my abilities.

"Okay," FoxyJuhnson murmurs in a small voice.

We concentrate, uh, pretend to concentrate on the lesson for a while before he speaks, "I just don't want it publicised that I live there, in the castle."

"Fine."

"Who knows as of now?"

"You're looking at her."

That's when he turned his head towards me. His jumbled blond locks swayed, and his light brown eyes held surprise, which quickly turned into realisation, followed by a brief warm flicker I caught a whiff of before it faded just as quickly.

"You better keep it that way then."

"Or?"

"Or it'll be unfortunate that you'll lose more than just a fistful of your flaming tresses and an equine."

Now what is *that* supposed to mean?? I squirmed at him like a short-sighted suburban aunt until the bell rang a few seconds later. Without so much as a glance, FoxyJuhnson strode out, leaving me with a lot more questions than I had arrived with.

Daze linked his hands with mine in the corridor, drawing the attention of several girls in the psych class. My head told me to discuss FoxyJuhnson's weird take with him, but something stopped me. How much did I really know Daze? He seemed harmless but there was an air of judgement about him. He would also find out that I'd been talking to FoxyJuhnson despite his disapproval. Anyway, I can try to get to know Daze better and make a decision accordingly.

"Daze, is Fadil your best friend?"

Caught off-guard, he frowned. "Uhm, yeah I do talk to him a lot these days about some stuff. Then again, Caecilia knows a lot more about me personally."

"Daze. Whom do you consider to be your closest friend?"

He's being so diplomatic. "Eh, I can't live without either of them." He shrugged and smiled dreamily at me.

At my blank (but encouraging) stare, he continued, "When I need to chill, de-stress, and just discuss random crap, Fadil is my guy. But Caecilia is the one who'd held my hand and lent me a sympathetic ear when I've been at my lowest. So I need them both." How sweet. I wish I meant this much to someone.

Because of this Zaekhuru, I've never figured out when someone is really my friend or if they are simply under my influence. My last best friend in eighth grade, Emma, was used to me barely making eye contact with her so that no "accidental compliances" occured.

This was only because I had come clean to her. We were so young she didn't fully understand exactly what it meant, but accepted my peculiar behaviour as it was. Once, even when she was sharing something as sensitive as her poor financial condition to me, I had to listen with my eyes down, and it seemed like I was more ashamed than she was, even though all I wanted to do was to look into her eyes and tell her that it did not matter.

Caecilia pointedly ignored me and my 'hey' when I slid beside her in Philosophy. A few blinks later, I wished she had chosen to ignore me longer.

"You don't know Daze. I have known him since forever. You are playing with his feelings the way girls like you do. He may look like it, but he's not one of you. He is simple and vulnerable, like I am. If you cannot find someone else, sink your teeth into Fadil or whoever, but leave my Daze out of this," she spewed out in a monotone while staring straight ahead like she was possessed.

"Sink my what. Okay, first of all, ew. Secondly, in a man's skin? Ew. You do not have a say in the relationship I have with him, just like I stay shut about whatever one-sided childhood sweetheart telefilms you live in. Also, I see a brother in Fadil, so I'd be pretty annoyed if you suggested something that disgusting—"

Catching Mr Laabh's eyes, I shut my mouth just in time to avoid his barrage of questions. We sat simmering while the teacher went on about the relationship between philosophy and behaviour.

Undeniably, Caecilia deliberately disappeared during interval and rather than facing her cold personality, even though it meant Daze's company, I searched the crowds for Daciana's voluptuous tresses.

There she was under one of the trees, a guy with a swarthy face standing unnecessarily close to her, leering at her and mumbling something. My blood boiled, but Daciana leaned against the tree, unbothered, and even bored. Thank goodness at least she was looking away from the leechy boy.

My legs strode toward them purposefully. "Daciana! Come on, they're calling you for lunch."

Leechy turned towards me with an annoyed expression, distinctly less impressed by my appearance than he was by Daciana's. Sometimes it's okay to just look okay. Daciana flashed me a wide smile and wordlessly came over. "But baby—"

"Oh, freak off," she said as we left him eating dust.

"Anyone important?" I raised an eyebrow at her.

"No boy ever is," she replied.

We spotted Daze and the others actually sitting down to eat today. "You go ahead and have a seat; I'll bring food for you today." And off she ran.

Waving at the gang, only Fadil and Daze returned my smile. Caecilia stared daggers at me while Edie fiddled with her phone. When I slid in beside her, she looked up nervously and put her phone away. "Oh, I didn't mean to catch you off-guard Edie."

"Yeah, no, I was just watching some YouTube, haha." She definitely wasn't.

"No noodles? Are you not eating today, Ally?"

"I certainly hope not, because if she diets just a lil more, her cardigans are going to hang off her as if pinned by a clothespin." Caecilia giggled meanly.

This caused Daze to shoot her a frown which Caecilia accepted and remained silent thereafter. Before I could think of a comeback, Daciana slammed a tray of delectable sushi in front of me.

My uncertain glance prompted her to add, "Try the tempura rolls. It's the best menu St. Regis has to offer." I took her word for it and did not regret it even a bit.

Two mouthfuls of maki rolls later, I looked up to realise that Daciana was still on her feet while eating. Pulling her down to sit between Edie and me, I deliberately ignored Caecilia's raised eyebrows and Daze's stressed nose rubbing. Fadil cleared his throat.

"Uhm, sohhh we have a football match this evening after the riding and we'd like it if you girls would come to watch us."

Daze added, “For the motivation,” as we all giggled. I noticed how they had brought this up consciously while Daciana was sitting there with us, which meant she was included too.

“You’re free, right?” I casually asked Daciana so I could confirm it, in case she still has a doubt. Her eyes shone as she looked at me.

Directing her question at Fadil she went, “Are cheerleading miniskirts allowed?”

Fadil fumbled but Daze quipped, “Only if your legs are prettier than Fadil’s.”

At this point, Caecilia, clearly having had enough, furiously stood up with her almost empty plate and walked off. Daze looked after her, clearly in a dilemma, but then his noodles lured him back in.

Gabby greeted us with a hug at the entrance of our class. She smelled of mints and sported a dark turban today. “What’s the occasion?”

“You’re seeing the new manager of Risotto Culture; I GOT A JOB!”

All of us beamed. Edie timidly grabbed Gabby’s hand, her eyes wide. “Oh that’s absolutely wonderful news! Where is it!?”

“It’s at Bano Garden square, opened this week!”

“Wait, is it the Italian one with lots of vines on the walls or something?”

“You’ve been there! Wait till you check out the new and improved version vis-a-vis yours truly!” Edie quickly mentioned that we hadn’t seen the place yet, but we had redeemable vouchers for Saturday. She conveniently didn’t name Daciana and that slightly annoyed me. Her excitement, although, made it clear that the plan was on.

We caught up with Fadil and Daze in the corridor. Daze told me that Fadil had felt embarrassed about the “pretty legs” comment and was giving him the cold shoulder, or in his case, the *cold bulky trapezoid muscle.*

As soon as I took my seat beside Fadil in History, he erupted, "Mahn, why did he have to use that phrahse in front of all the girls! My cahlves are hard as rocks! Feel them!"

He thrusted his knee at me just as FoxyJuhnson was walking up the aisle. He paused, cocked his head at us, and furrowed his eyebrows. Fadil glared right back. This continued for a full seven seconds, with his knee still almost on my lap.

"Stahp leering at my legs, Gaylord."

"Don't patronise yourself, McThighNeck. I'd be way out of your league," FoxyJuhnson replied with a smirk tugging at the corners of his mouth.

Fadil leaned towards me. "See how he didn't refuse his title? This one's a gahg."

I slapped Fadil's thigh. "Stop using that word, you don't have the right to say that. Also quit using the word 'gay' as an insult if you don't use 'straight' as one, okay?"

"But being straight is normal..."

"Your normal isn't necessarily the other people's normal. I get my eyebrows plucked. It's normal for me. Is it normal for you? Well it should be, looking at your monobrow but well, it's not. So when a person is queer, it's because it comes naturally to them, like *not* being queer comes naturally to you."

Fadil harrumphed but didn't counter me, probably because the teacher had walked in already. On some impulse, my head turned and my eyes met FoxyJ's. His expression suggested some degree of admiration if I wasn't mistaken. Either that, or it was the face people make when they are about to sneeze.

Shackleton ice ship's history keeps most of us so engrossed in this period that we all are jolted back to reality from the tundra when the bell goes off. Fortunately or unfortunately, FoxyJuhnson and I turn to face each other at the same time when starting up the aisle.

"Pippi the liberator of the LGBTQ," he declared and gave me the sneezy-smile as he walked away before I could even process his tone, let alone form a reply.

Daciana passed me her water bottle in Anthro class. She responded to my curious glance with a few nods before handing the bottle to me. A confused sip revealed that it was Coke. We took turns taking a sip every five minutes, and I was so grateful for her. When the class ended, I waggled my eyebrows in Heath's direction. Daciana, though hesitant, went for it. "Heath?" she called out and offered him the bottle like she had to me.

Pretending not to notice the surprised grin he gave her, I caressed her shoulder as a *see you later* as I exited the room. FoxyJuhnson was striding from the opposite direction. He was still wearing the superior-than-thou expression, but his eyes lit up with a challenging stare when he spotted me. It's evident he hates me.

"Did I misunderstand or did you compliment me in History?"

"Figure it out, I really hope for your sake that you are not a bimbo."

See? "You won't even fit into the criteria because you aren't even pretty, just pretty rude," I spat the words and whizzed into the classroom.

Relieved to find Daze sitting in the back row, I immediately hurried over to him and practically collapsed onto the seat. Daze looked up, "You smell like a bakery!"

"I taste like one too!"

Yes Ally. When in panic, flirt. Not.

He immediately stopped scribbling in his notebook and slammed it shut, turning his torso towards me. Out of the corner of my eye, I noticed FoxyJuhnson glance at us for a second too long before sitting down. Let him know that I certainly am desirable and it is HIS problem if he disagrees.

Daze's flirty bright eyes bore into me. Without making eye contact I tried to diffuse the tension in the air, "We're still in the lab testing phase but we're promoting well, aren't we."

"I sincerely hope you're considering hiring taste experts because suddenly, I am one." We smiled to ourselves.

With great pains, I managed not to steal another glance at FoxyJ. The commerce lesson was interesting today as we discussed internet usage in commercial practices. Both Daze and I focused on the lecture as we were basically made up of the same cement urging us to prioritise our studies over any distractions.

At the final bell, FoxyJuhnson turned his head towards us and looked at me with an expressionless face. I imagine I'm giving him the same expression in return. We lose eye contact in the crowd. Thankfully. Catching up with Daciana, we decided to meet the gang at the time of the match so that we could change into our cheerleading outfits. Daciana's dad was there to pick us up in their magenta SUV. Mr Iharlotte had thinning hair and wore nerd spectacles.

"Won't you introduce me to your friend, Daciana?" He had an uneasy smile.

"Hello, sir, I am Ally."

Daciana seemed uninterested in our exchange and was staring out the window. "So Daciana finally found someone like herself."

"It's actually the other way round, Mr Iharlotte, I found Daciana's nature quite similar to mine."

Daciana's surprised eyes met with my honest ones. The SUV halted in front of a white bungalow with a grey roof and bamboo seats on the porch.

The main door opened into a dining area with benches and chairs arranged alike. Daciana quickly led me upstairs. Her room was gold and white and much classier than I imagined. A huge wide mirror, framed like a Persian window, served as the room's main attraction.

One wall facing the bed displayed four large frames of horizontally cut slices of trees. Upon my curious glance, Daciana tells me those were from her old home where she grew up. They had to move away to make way for the construction of some military training zones, and many trees were cut down.

Her closet was in pastels and quite organised. She asked me to pick something. "Don't worry, I have great cinching waist belts at my disposal."

A blue sweater dress catches my attention, and when I tried it on with the belt, Daciana seemed pleased with my appearance. I guess that proves the effectiveness of the cheerleading outfit. Daciana just put on a yellow shrug over her sports bra.

"I was just joking about the skirt. I'm not here to make a fool of myself when you have actually persuaded your friends to hang out with me."

"But you'd look amazing in it."

"What's the use when people just wanna look and never talk."

"Guys wanna talk to you..." I trailed off at her sideways glance because we both knew why guys came after her—assuming she must be easy because of her bold personality.

While we were leaving, Daciana told me I didn't need to make niceties with her *step*father.

"I'm sorry, I didn't know that."

"That's okay, my parents separated when I was six, and I didn't ever miss him."

Daciana has had a complicated childhood, not unlike mine, and both of us are freaks in our own accords. Maybe that is the reason I found her easier to mingle with than Caecilia or anyone else. When we alight the stairs, Mr Iharlotte, closes his laptop and eyes us up and down before proceeding to retrieve the car keys.

"Don't cheer for the boys horizontally, if you know what I mean," he sneered.

"Just drive, man," Daciana spits back

After what feels like a long, uncomfortable silence, the familiar greenery of Blabamas' fields appears as a welcome sight. The gang greets us near the bushes, with three more of our male classmates who eye Daciana appreciatively, while a fourth one with slicked-back gel hair smiles at my bare legs. Gross. Daze, noticing their gazes, walks towards me and takes my hand casually in his.

"Come on, ladies, we have ice cream!" We sprawl on the grass and share tubs of chocolate crunchy and some kind of cookie and cream.

During the chit-chat, Daze catches my eye and smiles, running his eyes on me and nodding his head side to side; a gesture that seems to say I've done well for myself. Daciana saw this exchange and winked at me supportively. Every time Daze smiles at me, my insides turn to jelly.

Soon enough, teams are divided, and for obvious reasons, Edie and Daciana are cheering for Fadil while Caecilia joins me to spur Daze's team. "Do you wanna come up with a small step routine?"

"I already have one, thanks." Caecilia dismissed me.

"Well, would you mind sharing it so we can at least look like a team?"

"You're too witty not to pick it up on your own." Okay, so she was going to be outright hostile.

SIX

During playtime, I realised Caecilia's routine involved a lot of 80s ABBA disco flailing, followed by offbeat shouts of "Woohoo! GO DREAMERS! KEEP DREAMING, DRRREAMING DRRRRREAMING!" Yes. Daze's team is called Dreamers.

Once the boys started playing, I got so engrossed in the game that instead of cheerleading, I ended up being the flamboyant audience heckler. "WATCH OUT!" "GO FOR IT DAZEEEE!" "WoooooHOOOOOOOOOO"—accompanied by some hip waggling for luck. When Daze scored the second goal against Fadil's falcons (who had been leading by two), his eyes met mine at my *woohooooo* and he flashed that cute dimply grin of his. It made me feel like I was the only girl in the world.

Instinctively, I blew him a flying kiss which caused him to raise his eyebrows and widen his smile. Blushing, and very aware of Caecilia's eagle eyes on us, I had to clap and turn away. My delight at his scoring and playing really well wasn't an act so, when he scored another goal and brought the game to a tie, I found myself jumping with excitement. "You did it baby!" Yes, I had transformed into Elvis Presley in a woollen tunic.

Daze was laughing when, a few seconds later, the guy acting as the referee signaled for halftime and he jogged towards me almost immediately. I greeted him with a smile and a water bottle, but then

Caecilia shoved me aside and jumped into my personal space holding a towel handkerchief, and started wiping Daze's face.

When he saw my widened eyes, perhaps he got self-conscious because he took the towel away from Caecilia to do the task himself. Caecilia didn't take the hint.

She reached for his hair on her tiptoes, trying to push it away from his forehead and straighten it. The disgusting, sweat-soaked strands of once gorgeous hair. One swipe, swipe two, then a grab. Daze had grabbed her hand and shook his head at her.

Frozen, she pulled her hand back.

He walked towards where I had taken two steps sideways. Reflexively, I met his smile with mine though I didn't quite like what he did with Caecilia. "Ally, are you an ally of the Dreamers?" he teased, playing with my name.

"If they dream as sweetly as your footwork, then count me in."

We smiled some more. "Blue is your colour," Daze said, his voice semi-hoarse.

He went off to strategise with his teammates later. Caecilia stood nearby awkwardly. She dragged herself back to me as the match resumed. Wordlessly, she turned her head and looked at me. Fearing more spite, I kept my eyes on the game. With ten minutes left, the Falcons were leading by 5-4. One of Daze's teammates who had been sluggish the entire game suddenly started buzzing with energy.

And another goal! My body soared in the air so high that if I had boobs as big as Daciana's, they would have hitchhiked up and ambushed my face, no doubt. Five minutes left—we still had a chance to make the seesaw tilt our way. The ball was now in Daze's possession but Fadil tackled it away from him. With less than two minutes to go, Falcons took the defence positions. Fumble, fumble, the last minute. Daze attacks again, he's ploughing through the field with the ball between his feet.

Oh gosh, less than a minute left, I almost squatted in tension before I realised that my sunny yellow boy shorts would put the sunset to shame. Almost there, almost there—he kicks! He scores! WOOOOOHOOOO! The screams are unreal, and half of them are mine! There's a brief struggle, and then the whistle blows! Dreamers have won!

My body surged with excitement and didn't stop until Daze himself came running towards us, beelining straight for me and throwing his hands around my bottom and lifting me even higher!

We spun round, my fingers daintily gripping his hair at the base of his sweat-soaked neck to keep from falling; his laughing, hooting face staring up at me. For a few seconds, it was just me and him, and all I felt was but pure blissful joy. When his teammates came over, slapping backs and chanting 'Dreamers,' only then did he put me down and join the celebration. Heat rushed to my face, and Daciana laughed as she hugged me too. The boys gave high fives to me as well.

It didn't stop at the high fives. Daze somehow ended up beside me as everyone discussed the highs and the lows of the match. Some questions were directed at me when they ended with, "...What did you think, Ally?" or "...Wasn't it so, Ally?" Many shining eyes turned to me, filled with (was that adoration?), including Daze's, which held something more. My hand stayed in Daciana's the entire time, and it felt like she was now truly a part of this clique too. The way she was so comfortable at pulling some legs, she deserved to be here more than I did.

As the sun began to set, it was time to go home. As much as I like Daze, the idea of bumping into his stale, sweaty self on the ride home wasn't exactly appealing to me. Edie must be thinking the same because she approached Daciana and me and asked how we were planning to go home. Daciana came to our rescue and offered all the girls a ride home (with her creepy stepfather). But where was Caecilia?

"Daze? Have you seen Caecilia? Where is she?"

In our excitement, we had somehow forgotten about her. Daciana claimed to have seen her when the match had ended but not thereafter. Caecilia wasn't answering Daze's calls. We were about to start panicking when Edie received a text back from Caecilia saying she was already home and would talk later. Hm.

"She's been acting quite attention-seeking lately." Observed Daze.

Daciana murmured, "She always has been." We girls piled into Daciana's car.

With Mr Iharlotte's dislikeable personality, each one of us decided it would be best not to let him see our places and planned to get off at some nearby junction. Edie told me to get off at this monument known as Big House of Francis, as there would be plenty of conveyance options available for Bea-ansombo, the Keberkils' neighbourhood.

She got off first, and five minutes later, Mr Iharlotte told me I was next. He dropped me at the House of Francis, an old architectural wonder surrounded by a large market crossroad. I stepped out and looked around.

This place must be an older part of the town, if the leering gazes of the men and the disapproving stares from the women directed at my bare legs was any proof. People pushed past me, men with their elbows strategically out. Two taxis sped by without stopping. Next, a bus pulled up to a stop, but it wasn't headed to Bea-ansombo.

Fifteen minutes later, I was beginning to feel like SpongeBob in that one episode where he gets stuck at rock bottom. Even the PCO booth was across the very busy road with a dead traffic signal which I didn't possess the guts to cross.

A haggard middle-aged man with dirty hair and old shabby clothes seemed to have nothing to do but leer at me from a gradually closing distance. Soon, he was standing two steps behind me, leaning on a mobile screen protector vendor's stall and singing a strange song I didn't recognise. Now if I were to practise my Zaekhuru here, in front of all these people, no explanation would justify my grabbing his face and staring into his soul.

If he so much as tries to close this distance, I have made up my stance to punch him in the throat like Dad taught me. What will follow, I am not sure. Would I run like a lunatic on a tablet, or scream and attract a crowd. The crowd here didn't exactly appear like one to be attracted easily. A strange city, a strange juncture. Suddenly I found myself really missing Dad.

The song grew louder, and the pervert inched closer. Turning my head, I assessed his height to prepare for the punch.

"I didn't know you hung around here," a beanie-clad head addressed me.

FoxyJuhnson, of all people, stood there nonchalantly stuffing his mouth full of some kind of brown rice off a plate. The relief that washed over me at seeing a familiar face, even if it was my nemesis, matched the comfort he must have felt in his white tee and worn-out jeans.

"I want to go home." My voice sounded meek even to my own ears.

The hazy arrogance in his eyes vanished when he looked into my wide ones. Noticeably, the dirty pervert had taken a step back, keeping his gaze on FoxyJuhnson. A burly, grown man sporting a long stubble appeared to be accompanying FoxyJ. FoxyJuhnson deliberately positioned himself in a single stride between the pervert and me. The pervert backed a few steps away, and very quickly in fact, when the stubbly man frowned in his direction.

With a sidelong glance at me, FoxyJuhnson asked, "Where is 'home'?"

Maybe it was the tenderness in his voice when he said the word 'home' that suddenly I found myself trusting him with my well-being.

"Bea-ansombo."

He addressed the stubbly jaw tersely, "Get a cab."

StubblyJ nodded and set off at once, lost in the sea of people. FoxyJuhnson leaned against someone's scooter, his gaze focused again on his plate of brown rice.

"Where's soccer boi?"

This question filled me with exhaustion. Noticing my shoulders sag, he held one of his palms up at me before resuming stuffing his face.

Despite everything else going on my brain, it somehow still registers how tall he looks even while leaning sideways like that. His denims fit him snugly on the thighs; his biceps flex when he lifts the spoonful to his mouth; a sheen of sweat lightly lines his forearm. I shockingly find myself wondering—almost wishing—that his motorcycle is nearby.

He finishes his rice and hands over his plate with a nod to the vendor who takes it with a small bow. Huh, must be a regular, bringing in business too while he's at it.

Before I could look away, he turned his face towards me and as any normal human would, mistook my sultry stare for hunger towards food. He pointed at the vendor and raised his eyebrows. Shyly shaking my head, I took a step toward him. To my surprise, he closed the distance between us too.

"Did someone say something to you here, Pippi?"

He looked around beadily, squinting, and the effect it had was immediate as the onlookers promptly averted their gazes.

Words failed me as the jarring awareness of how delicate I was feeling consumed me all of a sudden. All that was left was for me to slip for no apparent reason and for FoxyJuhnson to leap forward and catch me in a dip, letting our eyes roam over each other.

But why was he widening his eyes at me? Wait. He had asked something. Shaking my head, I tried to avoid eye contact. He must not know how weirded out I was. There are enough creeps here already. Not that he is one, but he's not yet a friend either.

One of the vendors shuffled over, his eyes cast downward, and handed FoxyJuhnson a wad of cash. He took it wordlessly and pocketed it. Guess he doesn't bother keeping smaller bills with him, with the mansion and all.

The dusk was settling in. The streetlights lit up and the vendors switched on the tiny bulbs hanging on their stalls. Mum must be worried. Daze too. My stomach rumbled but the tension had killed my appetite. Many questions raced through my head: Did FoxyJuhnson come here regularly? Who was that stubbly guy with him? Where the heck was his bike and why couldn't he drop me home?

"Ask your model boyfriend to get you a metro card in case you don't have a penchant for being stuck in too many damsels-in-distress situations." FoxyJ smirked.

Before I could fully process this sentence, a cab screeched to a stop next to us, and Stubbly jaw alighted. The two looked at each other and exchanged some cryptic head nods that boys annoyingly do. With a sweep of his hands, Stubbly jaw directed me towards the cab's passenger seat. FoxyJuhnson blinked at me—reassuringly, somehow—and that was enough to spur me forward.

Just as I slid into the cab, stubbly jaw closed the door behind me. My eyes peered out the window, watching FoxyJuhnson walk around the front and bend to have a low conversation with the driver. Now any girl would think he might be instructing something shady, but at that moment—call it my instinct—I felt safe.

With one last glance, he straightened up and the cab pulled away. Unfamiliar markets passed for ten minutes before we exited a flyover and the familiar suburbs came into view.

"Tell me where to stop, ma'am," the driver quipped.

We drove for another two minutes until I spotted the hideous purple garden. Hastily stepping out, I asked about the fare.

"It's been paid, ma'am." WHAT.

"When? Who?"

"Mr Juhnson paid and left some extra tip too, ma'am."

"You know his name?"

"Everyone knows him, ma'am."

He drove away before I could process this, which became even harder as the sweet whiff of the purple pansies hit me and I realised the headache had resumed.

Daze ran to me as soon as I entered the front door. He grabbed me by the shoulders, "Where were you Ally? We were sick with worry!"

My mother sidled up to me too and smoothed a stray strand of hair before noticing what I was wearing. "Wait, WHOM have you been with? WHY did you ditch Daze like that? WHERE are your clothes?"

Mrs Keberkil saw her chance. "Girls these days wear their dresses way too short. They cross their legs and you can look up to their wombs—" Daze turned his head toward her with some menace.

Andrea met Daze's gaze undeterred, but thankfully didn't speak anymore. "Daciana's dad dropped me at the, this uh, juncture and I didn't know how to find my way here because it was too crowded for the taxis to stop and I didn't know—"

"It's okay." Daze, apparently my father now, cut me off, answering instead of my own parent who stood staring at me in dismay.

"You're home now, Ally, thank god. Are you alright, babe?" Daze's eyebrows were furrowed with concern and kindness and THE FUDGE, HE JUST CALLED ME BABE IN FRONT OF TWO OF OUR PARENTS. WE WERE PRACTICALLY MARRIED.

Eventually, I blurted out some form of consolation which satisfied both my "babe" referrer and my mother, and then I was allowed to retire to my room to nurse the migraine I was experiencing.

Before leaving, Daze bent down in front of me to meet my eyes and said, "Ally, please don't scare me like this again. You matter to me."

"You won today at the fields and I ruined the day for you, Daze..."

"You came back to me, my day is NOW made."

His smile was filled with such honesty that it moved me.

As the night fell, the smell of pansies became overwhelming. Sleep evaded me and the events of last evening lingered. What would I have done if FoxyJuhnson hadn't been there? Just how many men would I have tried to drop kick or Zaekhuru in the midst of a bazaar? Maybe Dad was right—I did have a tendency to believe I was invincible with this gift we shared.

After all, Dad hadn't been undefeatable. Some things would have to be changed. First, I'll be nicer to people, especially FoxyJuhnson and Caecilia. Second, I'll practice more Zaekhuru and head butts. Lastly, more humility, less overconfidence.

The sound of familiar male laughter roused me from sleep just as the first light of day streamed through the windows. An ear to the door gave away Fadil and Daze in the living room. Half an hour is all I had to wash and get dressed. Donning a beige and brown long sweater with my skinny dark Levi's, I decided that today was a low-key day. A side part in my hair was the finishing touch, and I made it in time.

"There she is." Daze smiled, eyes appraising.

My shy smile in return made Fadil look away, maybe causing him to feel like an intruder. Breakfast smelled heavy and sure enough, Hing Kachoris were waiting for me. Overwhelmed by the headache, I reached straight for the cereal bowl.

"You don't eaht, Ally?" Fadil quipped.

"Isn't that what I am doing right now?" I answered, my mouth full of milk and cornflakes. Fadil turned to Daze for explanation. "She doesn't like wholesome breakfast so early on."

The breakfast discussion shifted to this classmate of ours who had apparently been catfished. The girl he thought he was meeting turned out to be a trio of thugs who robbed him of his new flashy Fossils watch and the eight thousand cash in his wallet.

"Where did this happen?"

"Near Big Beer Pub," Fadil answered me.

"A sixteen-year-old minor called up to meet another minor for a first date in a pub and he found nothing suspicious about that?"

"Maybe he thought the girl was outgoing..." Fadil trailed off when I intervened, "There's a difference between being bold and having a death wish."

“This is my cue to get coffee so y’all can argue pumped up on caffeine.” Daze got up.

“Ally,” Fadil dropped his voice. “He got really worried about you. He cahlled me late at night and blamed himself fohr everything. It might not be my place to sahhy this but for his sake, be more cahreful with your adventures.”

He didn’t say it condescendingly or anything, so I simply gave him a slow blink as acknowledgement. Daze really was shaken up, huh.

We left for school soon after on his bike. If I leaned forward, our faces would be closer than they usually are at any time of the day, so I used this opportunity to try to console him about my well-being.

“You can relax about me. I am a big girl, Daze, and I know basic self-defence, thanks to my father.”

Daze scoffed. “How many people can one person sucker-punch at once?”

When we arrived, Edie greeted us in the shed, but Caecilia was nowhere in sight. Fadil was being a little touchy-mushy with Edie and she was clearly trying to avoid it—possibly because it was a bit too much PDA. I wasn’t sure if it was my place to ask her if she’s okay or not, but if I see it happening again, I will definitely intervene.

My thoughts were interrupted by a pink blur rushing toward me and grabbing me with a moan.

“Sis! I am so sorry! Stepdad is an a-hole! Did you reach home fine?”

“It’s okay, Daciana, there was some confusion but I made it home just fine.”

My narration of yesterday’s events went on for the entirety of our walk to the classroom. For reasons strange to me, I didn’t feel like divulging what safety waves FoxyJuhnson was radiating last evening, because it's not easy to describe it. Imagine walking on a tightrope, but with a chain tied to your ankle, so you know you won't fall even when you lose your balance.

Daciana's excited commentary continued throughout the entire Economics lecture.

"Was he smoking? He would look cool if he were smoking wouldn't he?" "This whole scene gives me a fookin *Peaky Blinders* vibe!" "Speaking of which, Heath would look rather dashing drinking some whiskey, me thinks!" Now she was even picking up a British accent.

"What are you guys laughing about?" Daze joined us in the corridor.

"Yesterday—" I squeezed Daciana's hand. "Yesterday I slipped in the bathroom, and I won't tell you any further details, ta-ta!"

Daze gave me a giant smile. "I really look forward to the classes I have with you, Ally." My blush would not quite express how my brain changed state from solid to liquid.

"See you in about forty, then!" Here's to hoping the smile I returned to him didn't seem as plasticky as I felt.

WHY DO I GET SO SHY AROUND HIM.

There was a small crowd of students debating near my seat in political science, blocking the path. The discussion seemed way too heated so I waited... and waited...

"Move it. Take it elsewhere."

FoxyJuhnson's deep, heavy voice cut through the high-pitched chaos. Some people listened and started to disperse, but two guys in particular totally ignored him. He looked dead serious—quite a contrast to his deep yellow Hawaiian shirt and flip-flops outfit.

It was obvious he came here straight after a shower, with the ends of his hair still damp and the top two buttons of his shirt undone.

After giving both the guys a generous ten seconds, he placed his palm on the shoulder of the bulky white guy wearing a skullcap.

The guy's immediate reaction was to shrug it off, but FoxyJuhnson's palm remained firmly clasped to his body. Watching bulky guy's right-hand form into a fist and his teeth clench, I knew it was Zaekhuru time. Quickly, I stepped in front of him and thrust my face in his personal space.

"You won't punch him. Go. Now," I said quietly.

He blinked. "What?" he blurted, incredulously.

FoxyJuhnson lifted his hand and gave the guy a pat on his back as if to say 'keep it moving,' while looking bemused.

Skullcap was still honking to his mate, "Bro, why that chick all up in my face like that? Who she?"

Wait, did he not get hit with the Zaekhuru?

He should not be reckoning this!

"Why so intense?" FoxyJuhnson smirked at me as we successfully took our seats back. Perhaps my headache was messing with my concentration and that's why the hypnosis was so weak that he was still conscious in the process. FoxyJuhnson was still looking at me when I realised I hadn't replied. His pale amber eyes bore into me and I made the mistake of looking back at him before any words had formed in my mouth.

Might I just practise Zaekhuru again? Okay Ally, focus. I closed my eyes and directed my gaze towards him with a new vigour. His irises shifted. Dear gosh, why the heck was his stare so sultry? Let's go with something basic.

"You will tell me your name."

His lips parted, a momentary frown.

"Why?"

Huh. This isn't how it's supposed to go. No cross-questioning in Zaekhuru! Shikerdoodles! It has malfunctioned! I have malfunctioned!

My frown and immediate shifting back made him sit up straight too. He didn't stop looking at me.

"Why are you being intense and ordering people about, Pipps?"

Maybe it was because he called me Pipps that I ended up blurting out, "Did you not feel compelled to tell me your name when I told you to?"

Now, I couldn't meet his eyes, but he had no problem turning his whole torso to face me.

"Because we're FRIENDS, huh?" he exclaimed, on the verge of laughing, clearly enjoying this.

He didn't let it go for the whole period. Every now and then he would glance at me and squint; nod his head interrogatively and wiggle his eyebrows. Trying my best to glare at him, I acted like I was keeping my cool, completely unbothered by how cute he looked when he was in a playful mood.

At one point, he actually whispered, "What's your secret?" but he had a slight smile on his face so I doubted he knew. When the teacher stood up to leave, so did I.

Embarrassed and confused, I didn't look back as I started to walk, only to be blocked by his body right in front of me at the end of the column. There was no space to get around him and he stood rooted like a wall. Forced to look up into his flickering golden eyes, I tried to read them. Gentleness.

"It's Aaron."

He held my gaze a few moments longer, wordlessly, before making his exit. Oy. Aaron Juhnson. Aaron. Wait, does he have a double 'A' like I do? This is exciting.

Possible Zaekhuru victim/Lab rat #2, Daze came to collect me halfway between classes. “Isn’t it just the perfect weather to go out?”

Daze pointed at the clouds, skies and the slight breeze. Grabbing this chance, I stepped in his path and made him look me straight in the eyes.

“Let’s skip Psych and go to the canteen!”

Concentration was complete, induction was throughout. Nothing changed in his eyes.

Then he frowned. “Good idea, but don’t you think it’s too impulsive?”

Fudge nuggets in the holy oven! I think I have lost my special ability. Just like that, without a warning. How? Maybe my mother was right, I should have respected it more and treated it as a gift when I had the chance. So now, are we happy or sad that this happened? Because it also means I have stopped being a freak.

I mean, partly.

Psych class went by in a bedlam. Daze was probably chattering about how they’ll be serving Hakka noodles in the canteen today, much to his delight, but all I could think about was trying to figure out the reason why my Zaekhuru seemed to have disappeared so abruptly.

“I haven’t seen Caecilia today. Wish her a good morning on my behalf when you see her.” Daze pats me on the back as he jogs off to his next class.

Huh. He can do that one himself. Weirdly, Caecilia wasn’t at our seat when I reached Philosophy. A quick glance around the room revealed she wasn’t there at all. A few minutes later, a girl with an unusually high ponytail in the last column waves her hands and catches my attention.

She points at the windows when I look at her. When I look out, I see Caecilia standing on the street below! Is she skipping the class? She answers my silent, questioning look with a 'come-on-over' gesture. 'HOW?' I mouth. She insists, her body language pleading.

It must be an emergency. But why is she calling me and not Daze? Must be some girls' thing. She already was extremely offended yesterday, maybe I should extend my friendly hand this time. Thankfully Mr Laabh ambles slowly, and I manage to slip out of the classroom before he enters.

Daciana once showed me a shortcut next to Fr Vindu's office which led to a small clearing at gate number two, where there were no guards. Maybe I can make a quick excursion and find out what's wrong and make it back in ten? Hmm. The coast must be clear because Fr Vindu's white habit is easy to spot, flowing like a 19th century British damsel's skirt near the auditorium. A quick peek confirms it: the hallway is empty. Thank god I chose to wear sneakers and not heels today.

There's a large iron gate which is padlocked, but the small door embedded in it is just latched. The biggest risk now is the latch making a horror-movie noise. I lift it gingerly, and although it squeaks, it's not loud.

With careful, slow movements up and down, I slide the door open to... FREEDOM.

Where's Caecilia? I spot her standing all the way down at the end of the school premises now. Glancing back, semi-jogging, I make my way towards her. She waves at me, her expression alarmed.

SEVEN

As I reach her, she's nervous and sweating. "It's Daze's mom! Come, quick!"

We're running towards... towards an ambulance! "WHAT? THEN WHY'D YOU CALL ME AND NOT HIM?"

"His classroom is in the L wing at this hour! I went to pay her a visit to talk about things, you know? I didn't feel like coming to college today, but no one opened the door so I called emergency and—"

The doors of the ambulance flew open, and a guy jumped out. Before I knew it, I was being pulled inside by him.

My natural reflexes kicked in and so did I—kick, I mean. Darn, I should have worn heels. My sneakers connected with the guy's knees and he groaned but didn't let me go. His elbows were locked under my arms in a death grip I couldn't escape.

Caecilia climbed in voluntarily (!!!!) and closed the doors shut before my shout for help could reach out. It's actually not an ambulance at all inside; we're on the rubber mat of a carriage van which started moving as soon as the doors locked.

My long painted nails scratch the man's neck before he pulls out an actual REVOLVER and pushes it to my forehead! It's not like I haven't seen one before, my dad had one too, which was larger than this one, but he didn't pull it out in front of me much and never taught me how to use it either.

He believed it wasn't necessary to spurt out blood when a few bruises could do the job or better yet, an eye-to-eye conversation in our case. Christ Fudgecake, this was the worst possible time for my Zaekhuru to have faded away.

It's time to calm down and assess the situation. Okay, so the van is being driven fast. What are the means available around me? Dirty pieces of clothes are scattered about, probably used to wipe grease or other human filth I'd rather not imagine as there is plenty of space for two people to lie down where I am currently sprawled with HALF OF MY UPPER BODY IN THE MAN'S LAP WHAT—I try to sit up but the bearded man pushes the gun's barrel further into my skin.

"WHAT THE HELL ARE YOU DOING?" My yelling makes Caecilia look up from where she's straddling my feet, trying to bind them with a thick, coarse rope.

"I'm making you disappear—"

Beardo thug shouted to interrupt her, "HEY! SHUT UP!" His face isn't in my line of sight but the expression on Caecilia's makes it clear that she shouldn't have answered me.

"Are you REALLY thinking Daze, Edie, and Daciana won't come looking for me in the next few minutes!?"

"Oh they will. They will search for you for days in fact, before they realise you've disappeared into the ocean—AH!" She's cut off by the thug flicking a dirty rag across her face.

"YOU WILL NOT SPEAK *ANOTHER WORD* NOW. UNDERSTAND?" The question was rhetorical.

My legs are bound, but there seems to be some wriggle room. I don't dare move though and make it clear that I won't. This is when I start spouting a stream of abuses at both of them. Finally, after I call the thug "Toby from *The Office* looking arse," he slaps me. Hard. Caecilia jumps too.

"Don't, uh, leave fingerprints on her skin more than necessary," she volunteers. To scare me, I am sure. And it works to shut me up. A few seconds later, that rag zooms in until it's tied around my eyes.

"I don't even have insurance," I mutter helpfully.

It feels like we've been driving for a bit less than half an hour, though I can't be sure because the experience feels like it stretches on for a tumultuous hour. The thug speaks as the van slows to a halt, "See, betch, this area is secluded so your cries won't do you any good and will only bring a kick to your gut from me with no living person around to hear you, so you choose."

The choice is made and I whimper as I'm manhandled; half carried, half dragged from somewhere sunny and grassy to somewhere cold and musty. My bound feet make sounds on stone paths and my hair gets caught on the rough edges of the walls.

Then there are stairs to alight. The way I'm being steered—half jumping, half stumbling—makes me think I might be spiralling downwards. Is this a prison? Once or twice I plan on falling down and pulling the thug's weight down with me, but if he falls upon me, I'll be the only one injured.

Bumping and struggling, It takes us several minutes to reach the landing. The cold air hits me at the surface, and I hear the soft click of a beaded curtain as we pass through it; it reminds me of strip clubs. Oh gosh, what if they've brought me to some sort of underground strip club and a place with God knows what kind of paraphernalia?

They will soon be put off by my boring nude bra and black and white boy shorts—WHY IS MY UNDERWEAR ON MY MIND WHEN I MIGHT HAVE BEEN TRAFFICKED!

Suddenly beardo thug slams into me from the side like a WWE move. He doesn't fall on top of me, but his weight drags me down and I scream as we fall onto something soft. A mattress. The smell of an earthy perfume hits me before I feel Caecilia's bottom land on my ribs. She's not heavy, so I can still breathe, although I pretend I can't. Her fingernails dig into the skin at my neck. "STOP. SCREAMING."

Beardo says in a muted voice, "Don't you now leave nail marks or bruises on her body."

As soon as she retracts her hand I inhale and muster the energy to lift my knee to my torso with a jerk and kick her in her back. She stumbles forward, her body landing on my face, but there's a satisfying thud as her head likely collides with mister thug, who reaches me in time to grab my forearms. Her body is immediately lifted off me and mister thug holds my forearms above my head so tightly that it hurts.

"You're bruising my hands, arsehole!"

"Here! Bring it around from the other side!" The thug instructs loudly and I hear Caecilia running and humph-ing.

I feel something cool and plasticky around my wrists. "Screw it tight!" The clamp-like thing tightens.

What the hell!? Convinced that I'm being racked like the medieval times, I start blurting out whatever frantic thought that comes to my mind, like:

How I'm going to pull and give myself black and blue marks around my wrists;

How I'm going to scream red murder;

How I'm not wearing the appropriate underwear for a sexy party!

Without warning, my legs are spread apart. Caecilia is widening the gap between my ankles.

"Wow, Caecilia! If you were interested in me, you should have just confessed instead of resorting to this underground trickery!"

Instead of saying 'trickery,' I used a curse that sounds similar. Similar clasps were fastened around my ankles. Spread-eagled on a mattress and blindfolded in some prison's basement, I awaited my fate.

Naturally, I broke into a cold sweat when I heard their receding footsteps. "WAIT! HOW LONG ARE YOU GOING TO BE AWAY!? WHAT THE HELL DO YOU WANT!?"

I might as well have been talking to a wall. Two minutes later, there is complete tangible silence. My eyes are blindfolded, my limbs bound, leaving only two senses: smell and sound. It smells like old buildings with a trace of vanilla scent near my head, perhaps a remnant of Caecilia's perfume.

My ears catch a faint sound of internal plumbing. The only thing keeping me from screaming for help is the fear of attracting some unwarranted lurker or rogue who will definitely take advantage of a young lady bound before him.

How long will it be before my mother or Daze realise I'm not the suicidal type? I'd rather murder someone else than myself. My father was the calmest one in our family. And look where it got him. It looks like my feistiness is taking me somewhere similar.

My stomach rumbles after a while and I realise it must be past lunch time. The fact that I am absent must have registered on my two (2) well-wishers. It doesn't seem like I will be fed or given a drink while I'm held as a captive here.

The only time they will come back is to take me to the sea shore and let me drown. There is no way of knowing how long I have been thinking these miserable thoughts. Two hours? Five? Either the evening chill has not hit me yet or the room is too warm.

The urge to move my arms is unbearable but it's like I'm tied down on a stretcher, almost like a medieval prisoner. The ones Henry VIII used to punish his courtiers for suspected infidelity. My muscles will stiffen in an hour or two, and I'll wish for the end already. Oh god my prayers have been answered. Footsteps! Woah, quick footsteps!

"Caecilia?" I croak.

"Pippi?" the male voice exhales.

"Juhnson?"

What is he doing here?

"You're in this with Caecilia?" I choke out, shocked.

This is devastating, I haven't caused him any harm, and thought he was so cute. Why are good looking guys always the bad guys?

"Who's Caecilia?"

His footsteps are leisurely and slow. The lack of incredulity in finding his classmate tied like a dungeon slave gives him away; he must be aware of something. Um, also, why else would he be here?

"Do you think I'm a fool?" I shout.

"You sure do look like one."

His voice sounds close to my head. Oh no, he's going to wring my neck or something. My breathing quickens, and soon I'm gasping for air.

His fingertips are on my cheeks. Really, this is when he wants to pinch my cheeks? He can choose to do just about anything right now and he decides to pinch my cheeks? Not even the cheeks on my back but on my face? Aaron is a weirdo, as if I already didn't know that. No wait, he's… lifting the blindfold off! Oh god, it's so bright. His face is upside down. Long bangs hanging off his forehead, his lips are parted and eyes full of confusion. Blinking rapidly, I manage to mutter, "Hi."

Unbelievably, he blew away the stray hairs that had escaped my forehead in the struggle today and were poking me in my eyes. He blew them off my eyes with his mouth. This bloke who goes around walking like an anime character with a dark history and threatening eyes, a blade hidden in his shoes, is pulling a modern-day Mr Darcy.

"What have you gotten yourself into, Pippi?" he breathes, his voice as soft as when it was that day at his place, when he stood very close behind me.

"Caecilia..." With no idea where to start, I was still trying to assess the situation. So, he's not in cahoots with Caecilia and the thuggy man.

Then WHAT in the world is he doing in this stone-walled room? Is he perhaps following me? Fatigue overcomes me. Juhnson seems to take the hint and moves. But where? One blink, and he's kneeling between my, uh, spread legs.

"EXCUSE ME??" I exclaim. With just a grunt in response, he freaking leans over me, his hands going to the clasps on my wrists.

Although his body does not rest on mine, I can feel the heat from his khaki bomber jacket. His Adam's apple is jutting out directly in front of my eyes. My lungs catch a single whiff of oceans and soap from his neck before he lifts his torso and places one of his knees beside my torso, shifting upwards.

Now I will spare the details of which part of his body is once again staring me in my face, too close for comfort.

Folding my wrist, he jerks my palm upwards so that the chain attached to the hand clamps to jangle.

It starts to make sense then—my hands are attached to a single link chain which runs beneath the mattress. All that time I was trying to break free, I was just fighting my own body force. He has pulled the chain up, freeing it from the mattress. Gosh my arms ACHE, what a relief. Quickly, I shifted downwards and realised my feet were also tied to a chain. What's left now is just getting these BDSM paraphernalia off of me.

"I don't have the keys to this, as you must have already guessed," Juhnson says, looking down at me.

"Where are we?"

He looks around the room. "This used to be a basement attic for us, but we don't use it anymore."

Us? Wait. THIS IS HIS PLACE?!

"So you ARE IN CONNIVANCE WITH CAECILIA!"

Juhnson glares at me, "Yeah Pippi, that is why I helped you out of your spreadeagle stance. And who is Caecilia anyway?"

"How come you didn't know I was here? And all of a sudden, why'd you decide to pay a visit to this attic you claim you don't check anymore!?"

Juhnson frowns as he looks down at me, sitting on the edge of the mattress, chained like a fugitive from the stone ages. "Your hair."

My shackled hands reach consciously to feel my bun. Pretty sure my hair is a frizz fest after this mishap. His eyes are on my chains which rattle with this movement, and he clarifies, "There was a lock of red hair wound up at the entrance of this dungeon and it happened to have caught my eye, luckily for you."

"Luckily for ME? What explanation would you have given when my dead body would have started to rot and stink up your home?" My voice is on the edge of hysteria.

We realise at the same time that I am now unable to make light or logic of this situation. He suddenly bends down and grips my shoulders, which seem to disappear in his large hands. Having pulled me to my feet, we both realise that my knees are shaking. The cause could either be the cold, the shock, or both.

"Would you be able to walk?" His voice has lost the mocking edge now.

Taking a wobbly step, I imagine alighting the endless stairs with these heavy chains. Ashamed, I shake my head in refusal. It doesn't take Aaron one second before he slips one arm behind my knees and scoops me up sideways in his arms.

His khaki jacket is what I fix my eyes upon, too overcome with shyness to look at his face. He smells clean, and his other arm goes beneath my back and settles at my arm. Without a word, he starts walking almost immediately like I weigh nothing more than a basket of fruits.

We pass the bead curtains and start climbing as I try to figure out where exactly to place my cuffed hands. My answer hits me when Juhnson involuntarily tilts my body closer to his for a better grip. In lieu of something to hold, my fingers spread themselves on his chest. He's warm and his chest feels tight, like he's packed smugly beneath. An urge to see his skin pulses in my brain. The chains on my feet rattle against each other with his every move.

What will his househelp, his maids say when he appears with a chained lady in his arms!? What about his parents??

"You are giggling because…?"

Aaron is lightly frowning at me and I let my head fall back as I imagine what a sight we must be. When I lift my head back up, his eyes are fixed on my bare neck. Oh Gosh, what if he's a vampire or something. He certainly checks off the list: lives in a castle; has a dungeon with BDSM paraphernalia; cold attitude; carries weapons on his person; has disapproving maids, etc.

Some of his locks have fallen over his eyes as he continues to stare at me. His gaze doesn't make me uncomfortable. If he had bad intentions, he had me fully vulnerable just moments ago. Subconsciously, I brush some hair off his eyes. Momentarily, he closes his eyes, and his face looks so serene. Hardened features relax beneath my fingers, which, on their own accord, trail down to the light scar beneath his left eye. The spell is broken. He opens his eyes.

Although I expect him to comment on my, uh, impudence, he surprisingly doesn't, and maybe it's my imagination but his eyes seem softer now as they meet mine. The sound of furniture being dragged reaches my ears. He slows, and we finally come to a halt.

It's the landing. He steps out and we're greeted by cool air, dark cloudy sky and the smell of trees mingling with algae-flavoured water.

"Where will you take me now?" My voice is barely audible under the hot-guy-botherosity syndrome.

"To my bedroom," is his calm reply.

My breath catches and I start coughing.

"Shhhhh!" he hisses.

He puts me down on my feet before the familiar front door to his house. So the dungeon was on one side of his place. With a key produced from his jeans pocket, he unlocks the door and we rattle inside. The noise my chains make is like the clatter that must have surrounded the Titanic's engine room. Juhnson huffs in annoyance, then bends down and picks me up in his arms again. Although I don't feel like complaining, it is only dignified that I do.

"Hey! I can—"

"No, you can't. You'll bring the butler, house maids, footmen, and the drivers in tow if you start parading with that four-piece band you're wearing."

He's light on his feet as we pass the great hall with French windows without anyone in sight. Near the stairs, he adjusts me against his body once again. Deliberately, I let my hands spread over his chest again.

"When did you last eat?" His voice is soft again.

"Breakfast." Exhaustion overcomes me. He looks at me, his amber eyes empathetic.

After several turns on the carpeted stairs and floors, he sets me back on my feet again. I realised we must have reached his room. Using another key, he opens the door, and I follow him in darkness until he shuts it behind us and switches the light on.

The room is small and congested, with grey walls, one of which was covered in graffiti, written something in a foreign language but in the English alphabet; a large dartboard with darts en pointe; grey and olive linen on bed with excessive amount of pillows; A Saturn moon lamp sits on the nightstand, with a hole on its surface?? A thick journal rests on top of a big wooden chest. His TV is the biggest I've seen in my life and the only thing bigger than that in the room is the window which faces an upholstered bench.

"Don't!" he exclaims, stopping my trudging towards his bed. And it's hard to admit it, but it hurts my feelings. He pats the bench as he kneels in front of it, opening the chest. Whatever, I won't accept his offer now. His rummaging through the chest makes it clear that there are sorts of heavy metal tools inside.

My eyes wander to the journal he's placed on the bed. It says 'private' on the cover, written by hand. Aaron never struck me as the journaling type—next, he'll be telling me he collects stickers too.

"Shouldn't you be sitting down for this?"

He's holding what looks like a set of *very* long pliers. Shaking my head, I hold my hands out and trudge a few steps towards him. He cocks his head before coming closer, pliers first, clamping them onto the chain between my hands.

His muscles flex as he squeezes the handles, and I have to admit, his biceps are somewhat a work of art, especially when they pop out beneath two layers. Seconds later, I'm free! Both of us stare at my shackled feet now.

"Sit," he sighs and points to his bed.

With some smugness, I plonk my butt on his olive-green bed. He kneels on the floor with one knee before me.

"Can you lift one of your legs up?"

"Is that the position you like?"

The words slip out before I can control my mouth, and I cringe in horror.

Aaron freezes for a moment before lifting my right foot and resting it on HIS SHOULDER. His eyes narrow, a subtle smile playing on his lips like butter won't melt in his mouth. With a quick snap, he releases the last chain too, making me lose my balance and fall on his bed on my elbows.

He stands quickly, "I'm getting you some water. Do you want something to eat? It's been, what, nine hours."

The mention of food reminds me of my bladder. "Where's the washroom? And yes, some water would be great. I don't feel like eating just yet."

Turns out the bathroom is outside his room, across the hallway. It's all white and meant for two people. Two mirrors, two towels, and so on. There's a Bose speaker in one corner, and brands like

Park Avenue line the aisle. Everything is pristine. Juhnson is loaded. When I exit the washroom, I almost walk straight into him, waiting outside the door.

He hands me a bottle. "Your family must be worried. Here, call them and let them know you're safe and on your way home. I'm making it very clear that you are not to mention that you were held at this place."

There's a small 00s-style handset in his hand which appears to be brand new. "That's not your phone, is it?"

It's definitely not his phone. After downing a few grateful gulps of water, I take the phone and dial Mom. Aaron leans against the wall, lost in thought, but doesn't give me privacy.

"Mom?"

She gasps, "AALIAH. Oh my gosh, baby, are you okay? Where are you?"

"Mum, I'm fine, I think someone mistook me for someone else and kidnapped me, but I am not hurt."

"KIDNAPPED YOU?? WHAT DO THEY WANT?? WHERE ARE YOU!?"

Daze is also shouting in the background.

I try to calm her down. "Mum, they don't want anything, they have released me. I'm taking a cab and coming back, keep the fare ready."

"Honey! Daze will come to collect you, I'll come with him, tell us where to be!"

"That's the problem, Mum, I don't know where I am. Don't worry, I can see the road, and I'm definitely in the city. I'll take a cab. I'm coming, okay?"

"Please come soon, Ally. We're waiting for you." She's still breathing—thank gods and thank heavens—when I disconnect the call.

Aaron is smiling at the floor with his eyebrows raised. "Do I look that bad?" My outstretched hand holds his handset.

Juhnson pockets the phone and steps into my personal space. He fingers my stray hair. Wait no, that doesn't sound right. To put it differently—he tries to tuck the stray strand of hair back behind my ear. It doesn't feel as sexy as they make it look on TV, but it sure does feel filial. I look up at him and there's empathy in his amber eyes, along with something else I cannot recognise.

"That should do," he abruptly declares and starts walking towards the end of the hallway.

My passive-self needs some encouragement, which he provides by pausing midway and turning to widen his eyes at me till I saunter over. We pass a butler who stands to attention and asks "Sir?" to Aaron in a low voice. He suffices the explanation with just a head shake, and the butler immediately orders someone through his earpiece to open the garage.

"I've told Mum that I'm taking a cab..."

"Don't be silly, I'll put you in a cab hundred metres from your place but you are NOT leaving here alone."

There's a doorman by the front door to whom Aaron instructs, "Adidas, black." And we continue walking. Where did all these people come from? How exactly important and rich is he? He pulls out his all-too-familiar red Apache. Recalling all that stretching I had to do last time to avoid, by default, sitting half on his back, I feel the exhaustion catching up.

My thoughts are interrupted by a footman fetching a folded black piece of clothing. Juhnson retrieves it and hands it to me. It's a men's tracksuit jacket. For me? This is surprisingly touching, it's actually considerate of him.

"Don't you have any other motorcycle that doesn't tilt its seat almost vertically?" Using my arms as a shield over my Adidas jacket-clad bust, I let my weight fall on him.

His shoulders feel sturdy and dependable. Putting his helmet on, he responds to my question with an unrelated statement, "Put one of your hands on my waist, or your back will bear all the resistance."

Not needing any further prompting, I comply. Needless to say, my body moulds to his. For a second, neither of us moves.

Aaron glances at me sideways and offers me a very nice smile, one he doesn't elaborate. He drives at a speed that's a bit faster than comfortable, so I'm thankful for his jacket. The advice on my posture turned out to be correct because now I'm not bumping chest-first into him every time he hits the breaks. We won't mention that I'm already positioned as though we're a single unit. At a red light, he asks if I'm okay. We reach familiar streets quicker than the last time.

He asks me to wait by the bushes while he tries to flag down cabs. The suburban streets are shrouded in darkness, with a few isolated lampposts casting faint light. His hair falls on his face in such a way that it's not possible to read his expression.

"I still don't get how this random guy knew about your basement and that it was kinda uninhabited."

Juhnson pauses and replies in a steely voice, "James fort has been there since 1361 and was once the palace fort of Al Nustansir the Second. Even sixty years ago, caliphs from Egypt gathered here for meetings so it was always a public affair.

"There are still parts of the fort I have not been into, and rooms which some historians have visited but my family hasn't. I hope that clears up your doubts, Pippi, and if this doesn't, feel free to believe whatever helps you sleep at night."

Woah, he got obscenely offended. "Don't snarl at me, I was held hostage at YOUR fort since, what, 12 p.m.?"

He started nodding long before I'd finished. "Right. Yeah. You've had a tough day. HIYA!" A taxi finally screeched to a halt in front of us.

Because of the last time, I knew Aaron would handle the directions. When he gestured at me to get in, he murmured, "I'm gathering the fare would be taken care of? Because if I pay, you'll have to change your story about where you got the money from."

Nodding absentmindedly while unzipping the Adidas, I tried to decide how to thank him. Anything could have happened—from my sneaker floating in the ocean to my new slave name being Neetha—if he hadn't been there. Our eyes met and I tried to convey as much gratitude as possible through my expression.

"Don't fall for my human acts, Pippi, I am definitely not the good guy in anyone's life."

Click. The door shut.

Of the car, of my hopes. Hopes of what? No, I don't have the answer to that.

A minute of wheels squeaking, and we were in front of the Keberkils' place. Daze was pacing about in the driveway and practically ran when my cab stopped. No sooner had I alighted than I was engulfed in biceps and the smell of summery aftershave. It was warm and it was caring and more welcoming than anything else at that point.

My mother came running next, the drama unfolding in front of the cabbie. Wiping her tears, I assured everyone I was okay. This was between Caecilia and me and I would deal with it that way. The version I told everyone was that I went out to the loo, saw a stray cat and followed it outside and ended up getting smuggled into a van.

No, I didn't see their faces but it was a couple and they were looking for a girl named Bava who apparently went to Regis Ruler as well and was supposed to be near the premises at that time.

Yes I was unharmed, just famished. "They don't know what they have gotten into, kidnapping the daughter of a police officer," Mum muttered darkly while spoon-feeding me delicious paneer tikka biryani. Thank god she was still waiting to inform Dad's friends that I'd gone AWOL or there'd be a whole troop of uniformed men running through the streets.

"You didn't tell anyone else, right?"

"Of course, our friends know Ally, Gabby was the first to look for you and that was after Edie and she had scaled the school fields.

"We decided to check on our usual hangouts before informing Fr. Vindu, so only the six of us know." Daze, Fadil, Edie, Gabby, Daciana and ...Caecilia. "Caecilia doesn't know yet." Daze continued when I realised I had spoken out loud again.

"She didn't pick her phone up. Heath knows too—you know that blond nerd whose name is always on the topper list? Daciana brought him along when she went to search the primary building area. Didn't know he was a friend."

Woah, look at Daciana go! Daze fetched my bag and I called Daciana immediately. Sobs greeted me and continued throughout the call.

"Daciana! Honey, please relax now, I'm fine! The kidnappers let me go as soon as they realised I wasn't who they wanted so no harm done!"

"You are the only one I have, Ally," she said. The resignation in her voice hit me. She really was such a genuine, caring person who was so misunderstood by our peers.

"Honey, I love you, you are my sweetest and possibly only friend here whom I trust. And hey! I heard! HEATH! What's the scoooop?"

"Ally! I can't believe you're asking me this after you were just kidnapped for god's sake!? I'll see you tomorrow at school! Also, just so you know, I'm not letting you out of my sight from now on. Bye-uh!"

When my head hit the bed that night, albeit the returned and renewed headache, I was not feeling any residual anger towards Caecilia. It was clear what I had to do. The next morning, when Daze knocked on my door, his jaw dropped as I greeted him with my hair down, wearing a blue wool dress with huuuuge pockets over my dark jeans, and my string of pearls and flat mules.

"Doesn't look like something happened yesterday, right?"

"Yeah, I mean, you've concealed it great, but I can still recognise the exhaustion in your eyes. You look pretty though, Ally."

We blushed. "I actually came to ask if you'd wanna stay home today, but you're ready to knock out!"

"Dad always said, 'When you want to change things, change yourself first.' So..."

EIGHT

Daze asked me to hold him tighter on his bike, and compliance was a pleasure. Nothing like the wind in your hair and cheek resting on the suede jacket of your crush. Fadil, Daciana, and Edie ran to us as soon as we pulled up at the parking shed. Two muscled arms encircled my waist and lifted me up way too high in celebration before my feet touched the ground.

"OOF, thanks Fadil!" He smiled as I gave him a hug.

"Get off you big brute! ALLY HONEYYYY!" and I was pulled to rest my head on her pillow-soft boobs encased in purple wool.

"Daciiii honeyyyyy!" Daciana burbled a handful of *missed-you's* and *thought-you-were-a-goners*, while Edie stood patting both our backs with a shy smile.

Our reverie was interrupted by Daze shouting, "Caecilia! LOOK! She's back!"

Only then did I notice Caecilia standing across the lane, back against the wall and mouth agape in a manner unlike someone who was supposed to not have known that I had been missing for half a day. It must have taken her a whole sixty seconds to process that she had to plead nonchalance.

Our group had already begun to saunter ahead so I didn't wait around to see Caecilia's reaction and nor was I much interested, to be honest. She tried. People have tried before. Zaekhuru protects me.

Admittedly, it didn't work yesterday and hasn't been quite effective this past week, but it still gives me confidence.

Daciana filled me in on how they had split into search parties of two for each building block, and had even skipped lunch and two other classes. Her 'beau,' as I had decided to call him, Heath, had also skipped his last class to help her as soon as he found out. "I didn't know who else to approach. Thank heavens he settled it there and then by offering to venture out with me."

They still hadn't exchanged numbers, but she promised me she'd tell him the news in person after Eco class. Next class was with Aaron. I owed him one.

"Pippi," came his voice from behind me in the corridor.

"Everyone, and I mean *everyone* is excited to see me today!" My grin was wider than I could control.

He rolled his eyes. His denim shirt was unbuttoned at the top, so the leather cord around his neck peeked out.

"Anyways, excitement is infectious."

"I'm vaccinated," he answered.

He wouldn't meet my eye and did not look ready for any small talk.

"You know what, Aaron, Caecilia's jaw was ON the floor when she saw me! I wish you could've seen the look on her face."

"What IS the deal between you two?" The inquisitiveness of the sentence did not reflect in his monotonous voice and his dirty blond head which was turned away.

"There IS no deal, especially now that she was planning to feed me to the sharks! She likes Daze and looks at me as a threat, is what."

"And is that why you threaten her as well?"

What?

"That jock strapper has been her friend for way too long, Pippi, and you've just waltzed in with your dainty nose, expecting to win him over in four days?! Fourteen years versus FOUR DAYS?!"

Have I ever seen Juhnson this passionate about anything?

"What makes you think I'm making any extra effort to 'win him over'?" I air-quote the words.

He rolls his eyes in response and sighs dramatically. His chest rises up and down in that shirt that looks way too snug, and I have to focus to keep my eyes on his face.

"You know what, why am I even interfering in your matter? Resolve it, make an offer he can't refuse or just pull out your big guns, I don't care. Just stay far from my house. Don't keep showing up at my door with an equine in tow or even worse, strapped in provocative stances in some underground store rooms!"

What's gotten into him today? He's in an even worse mood than usual.

"Which butler stepped on your toe today, master Juhnson?"

Aaron just leaned back in his seat, refusing to meet my eyes. Today's lesson on Aristotle was interesting enough that I behaved myself for some odd thirty-five minutes. But I couldn't leave with this bitter taste lingering between us, so I invoked Zaekhuru. Better to keep testing it as well, maybe it'll work after I've let it rest this long.

When I stood up and our eyes met, I willed him, "Don't be angry at me." His frown melted, and his eyes widened.

Huffing, Juhnson raised one of his eyebrows. "What... what right do I have upon you to do that?" he muttered before increasing the gap between us and backing off.

Jeez, my Zaekhuru was definitely not working. And why does FoxyJuhnson speak so ominously? The bitterness in my mouth got worse than raw coffee. My eyes automatically followed his retreating form, just to land upon the approaching one of Daze. Here's to really hoping I am not the cause of the glare that Daze shot Aaron.

Daze offered me his soft, suede-clad biceps, and I was more than eager to comply. His dimples really make him the most attractive guy in any room he walks into. However, not even his amusing recount of how his Business Studies teacher's severe cold made his pronunciation wicked—calling 'gentleman' as 'bentlemen' and 'cases' as 'gases,'—could take my mind off the small spat with Juhnson.

"You're still tired from yesterday, right, Ally? I told you, you should have taken some rest today."

"Resting aka lying in bed and thinking about what I went through? Nah, sorry."

Daze stopped meeting my eyes. "I'm always here with my sticky-out ears, eager to listen whenever you feel like talking, I hope you know that."

Gosh. He's the sweetest. Nodding, I took my seat. With everything that had happened, Daze was now friendlier and we were closer. Caecilia had managed to completely flip the results from what she had originally intended. She definitely would not try to intimidate me again, especially now that I also harboured her secret.

Caecilia watched us with flashing eyes when I let Daze carry my bag as he came to see me off in Philosophy. Completely ignoring her, I gave him my ToBT smile when he placed a reassuring hand on my shoulder before running off to his lecture. Ha! Nothing for her.

"Am I missing something?" Caecilia asks innocently.

Unbelievable.

I couldn't help but spit, "You missed your chance to requite your childhood love, is what." When I looked straight at her, something shifted in her eyes.

"You...escaped." Hah.

"No shxt, Sherlock."

"Who helped you?"

"A ghost. What does it matter to you, madam criminal?"

"Why haven't you told Daze yet?"

"Leverage, dumbarse."

"You. He will see through you someday."

"You still won't be in his tunnel vision ever."

"You don't even love him."

Mr Laabh stumbled in before I could reply. The freakshow didn't even bother apologising to me and just sat there, arguing without a hint of remorse in her eyes whatsoever.

The one who laughs last, laughs the most or something. "I've got the keys to your friendship with Daze so I'd watch it if I were you."

Yep, I let her have it before walking away. Daze caught up with me at the end of the corridor.

"You're following me."

"Shhh, don't let them know."

He played along. Lucky doesn't even begin to describe how it feels to have this gorgeous man search for your face in the crowd. It was also noticeable how he didn't pause for Caecilia who was but a few steps behind me.

"It's soya chunks Friday!" Fadil was ecstatic today. "I'm getting bowls ihn and y'all can dig in later."

Daciana shoo'd away the lurkers from her table as we settled in, with Daze and Daciana on either side of me.

"Will you all fill me in on yesterday?" Edie uttered demurely.

"There's nothing so dramatic about it. I was kidnapped..." here, I made eye contact with Caecilia.

"I escaped."

"But why did they kidnap you in the first place?"

"That's for them to know and for us to find out."

"They weren't aware of who they were kidnapping," Daze added, causing Caecilia to lift her head sharply.

Leaving her alone in her misery, I suppressed the urge to elaborate. Fadil was right about the soya dishes—each one was delicious.

"So, we are meeting tomorrow at that Italian café or nah?" Daciana quipped.

"Definitely," I answered as Daze uhhhhh'd and Fadil continued to chew.

One glance at Edie and I was able to confirm, "Edie and I will be there."

Fadil swallowed noisily before nodding. "If everyone's going then I will too."

"I'm not going, I have plans?" Caecilia guessed, looking at Daze hopefully, giving him an escape window.

He didn't miss it; he exchanged a glance with her before turning his gaze on me. All I had to do was shoot him my resting bxtch face and we had the whole gang minus one, meeting Daciana pronto. As Edie and I strolled to our next class, I tried to pry out some information about Caecilia.

"Do you think Caecilia cares about me? Like, with what happened yesterday and everything?" I tried to keep my voice as breezy as possible.

"Ummm, I'm not sure but it's just my uh, opinion, that her kind attitude maybe, comes and goes?"

Edie seemed to be thinking. "What do you mean?"

"She seems to be, um, zoning out from time to time today." Well. That was weird.

Edie's pace quickened as she spotted Gabby. "Gabbs, look who's lost and found!"

A very animated Edie recounted her version of my abduction to a scandalised Gabby. Trust them to not let the protagonist get a word in. Gabby was sympathetic, but most of her breath was spent applauding Edie's valour and presence of mind when she came up with the idea of asking the local vendors around St. Regis if they had noticed anything unusual. Maybe I'll have to agree that in Fadil's absence (or Gabby's presence?), Edie is quite rational.

Speaking of Fadil, he eventually caught onto me shooting glances at Aaron in History class, and grew suspicious.

"That dude gives me the chills sometimes, mahn. You too, huh?"

"Um, he's alright, I guess?" I responded.

"I've heard stories about him getting beat up by gangs, but then there are also ones where HE ends up injuring more goons."

"Yeah? When was all this?"

"It has always been this way ever since he joined St. Regis, maybe like two or three years ago? Always hanging around near Vinduz's office, that guy."

Juhnson's eyes were cool and unbothered, even when he did return my glances. To be honest, even I'm not sure what I want from him. Halfway through the lecture on the history of American mafias, I leaned in and whispered to him, "We good?"

"Shh, I'm trynna concentrate here." He didn't look away from the blackboard.

Huh. Fine. If I am being truthful, he did look super engrossed. When will I be such a swot?

His hand holding a water bottle blocked my path when I got up at the bell.

"Go on," FoxyJuhnson nodded at the gadget-like LED temperature display on the bottle in his hand.

Two unladylike gulps later, I held it back towards him. His fingers closed around mine in the exchange and there was a pause as I searched his dark eyes.

"What are you doing, Pippi?" His voice sounded weary and on edge.

What did he mean? Our quarrel? Zaekhuru? The uncombed state of my hair?

"Don't look at me like that. You are responsible for what happened."

He was continuously losing me with these cryptic phrases. Also, I did not like the accusation in his tone.

"If you want to talk in codes, Aaron, catch me at the end of the day."

I gingerly extracted my fingers and half-ran to a patiently waiting Daciana. What I will not accept from a boy is impertinence. Yes, he saved me from that dungeon. Yes he's cute. But it takes a lot more than that to get comfortable with me to make me feel bad about myself for no apparent reason.

Surprisingly, Heath was waiting at the door of the Anthro class with a smile. For the first time ever, I saw him smile genuinely instead of conceitedly. He nodded at me and grinned at Daciana.

"We secured the kid."

"Just the pet left now," he answered, still grinning.

Nuggets in fudge! They had an inside joke! Good for my girl Daciana. We waggled eyebrows at each other before we took our seats.

"Invite him to the café!"

"Oh! Do you think I should!?"

"DUH. We'll leave you two alone later and you can talk… and stuff."

"I never got to thank you for coaxing the guys to be there. Having at least a few guaranteed customers on day one will definitely look good."

"They would have come with or without my persuasion, they are just shy about their food habits in front of pretty girls." We avoided eye contact as we both knew that was not the truth.

"What really caused Heath to start speaking to me is the mystery of your disappearance, if we're being honest."

"What if the next time I pull this, you two end up on a date?"

"Babe, never do that, it's you over any boy, any day."

Daciana rested her musky, sexy-smelling head on my shoulder. At the bell for Commerce, I squeezed her hand before leaving her to have a chat with Heath. Daze was sitting on the stairs, deep in thought.

"If I plopped down beside you, we'd either block the staircase or get run over." He straightened with a sleepy smile.

"What would I have done if you had really been kidnapped?"

"You would have rescued me, of course?"

"Of course, and I would also have the blood of some thugs on my hands. Would you have paid me visits in the juvenile delinquents ward?" He flashed his delicious side smile.

"Hah, telling you in a sombre voice how your mother misses you every day. It would get boring after the first few times, won't it?"

"Those aren't the only visits allowed. There are conjugal ones too."

The blush that spreads across my face is far from attractive. With my face resembling the scarlet bottom of a baboon about to mate, I walk into Commerce and make eye contact with Aaron, sitting nonchalantly with his feet up on the last seat.

His natural frown seems to always make an appearance in my presence. Shaking my head more internally than externally, I prep for the class. This subject is tough for me, and I take diligent notes on C2C business throughout the lecture. At one point, Daze pushes a lock of hair behind my ear when I'm busy writing. Although I feel the touch like a spark at the back of my neck, I just give him a small genuine smile in response.

A few minutes later, his fingers caress the side of my temple again before moving to rest behind my ear. Before I can look at him, someone pretends to cough loudly at the back. Most students in the quiet class turned to shoot a glance at Juhnson, who's glaring at me. At us.

"Mr Juhnson, this is a very rude way to ask for water, don't you think? Fliza, would you mind sharing your water bottle with him please? The poor boy might faint from a dry throat after the coughing fit."

A beat passes before Aaron blinks at her, then excuses himself to go to the water dispensers. It doesn't miss my notice how he deliberately kicks Daze's bag when he passes us. Daze mutters a curse under his breath in response. All those fantasies about guys getting jealous over you? Yeah, no butterflies in my stomach—only caterpillars at the back of my neck. Besides, I don't actually think FoxyJ has any feelings other than annoyance for me.

Hurray, school's out for the day. Daze isn't pleased that I should be up for horse riding, but I am. However, I'm not getting positive vibes today, so I decide to back out. Edie joins me. She's experiencing the red tide, so we make a stop at this nearby café which has good pizzas. "You're closest to Fadil, aren't you?" They say you shouldn't speak while chewing, but I ask anyway.

"He's lived in the neighbourhood since we were kids. We used to play cricket together. He never made me feel like I was different from the other boys in our team."

She's a sportswoman? "You play?"

"How can I, when there's no girls' team." Edie drops the outer crust of her pizza slice onto her plate. This is new information.

"And you and Gabby? Does she live nearby too?"

Edie smirks at me. "I wish. Gabby is just a friend. She's really fascinating. Have you noticed how when she listens, she gives you her whole attention and hangs on to every word you say." She smiles.

My mother is waiting for me when I reach home, holding a cup of PANSY-flavoured tea again. Andrea makes it herself by grinding the tea leaves with Pansy petals.

"She said it calms your head." It looks disgusting.

"You've been having all these headaches lately, Ally, and we just want to comfort you."

Although it looks a sickening muddy colour, it's not worth refusing my mother's puppy dog face. Andrea watches me fondly as I gulp it down.

"Are you settling in okay, sweetheart?"

"Yeah, Mum. St. Regis is more diverse than my previous schools. And Daze—" He smiles as he walks in on us, just back from the stables, "he's been so supportive, showing me around and making his friends accept me so easily."

"Hey-hey I can't take credit for the gang liking you, that's all on you."

"Does even Caecilia like her?" Andrea pipes in.

Huh. Just a question, but my headache returns with a pang. A big one. Caecilia gives me a headache.

"Yeah, she likes her too, Mum. What a weird thing to ask."

Daze lies. We don't look at each other as I change the topic.

"Tomorrow we're going to this great new café on INVITATION since my *friend* Daciana is the manager."

Mum smiles. Andrea smiles. Daze smiles. My smile fades as I realise I have nothing to wear. Typical.

My morning goes by catching up on homework. The headache starts at random times when I focus, and then it gets hard to recall things. Somehow, I push past through it as I'm blessed with a higher IQ, thanks to my mother. Donned in my olive-green kaftan top with dark tights, hair loosely draped on one shoulder, I manage to make Daze check me out appreciatively.

Café Dentaurus is a wooden-deck-themed place painted royal blue and accentuated white and cream furnishings. Artificial tulip vines wind around the railings and not-so-artificial peace lilies sit in pots around the place. We climb the deck, and Edie spots Daciana inside almost immediately. She's wearing a navy-blue hoodie and a plastic chrysanthemum clipped on her hair as part of her uniform. Cute as fudge, but not as cute as her smile.

"HEY, you guys are on time!"

"Most of us," Fadil murmurs.

Caecilia isn't here. Well, I'd prefer if she stayed away from my friends.

"Daciana, I'm not even going to look at the menu—you order whatever you think I'd like and something cool to drink, prithee." Daze and Edie nod in agreement while Fadil settles for spaghetti.

"Count me out of the sheep too," Caecilia's snotty voice reaches us before she does. As expected, she asks for a chair to be placed between Daze and Fadil. Well, she can sit on his lap if she likes, and he still won't give her a second glance.

"Daze, remember when in class 7th grade we went for that picnic and sat in a wooden shack like this? Gosh, those were some peaceful days."

Daze nodded uninterestedly.

"Today is a peaceful day as well, Caecilia, don't you think?" I said. Yeah, she annoys me and so does this headache.

"We have seen better days, Aaliah."

"Yay, look, the drinks are here!" Edie is so cute trying to distract us from Caecilia's rambling.

"Banana dates shake for the boys and Belgian chocolate ones for my girls!" Daciana announces as a waitress serves us. The shake is delicious.

"All those who were making faces about coming here yesterday, what do you owe me now?" I teased everyone but Edie at the table.

"Why is the food stereotypically gender segregated?" Caecilia tries to make a point, cutting me off as usual. Did she forget that I can destroy her just by exposing her as the secret kidnapper in front of everyone?

Daze raises a toast. "Wouldn't have admitted it, but if Ally hadn't used her cute persuasion, we would have missed out on such great drinks and atmosphere. Cheers to Ally and Daciana!" We all raise our glasses to a bashful Daciana, hovering nearby at another table.

Fadil jokes, "Aw, bobo, you would have dragged your buhtt to heck if Ally used her *cute persuahsion*, also known as 'feminine vixen ways'!"

Narrowing my eyes at Fadil (and him reciprocating), I challenge Daze, "Tell him it's not true, Daze. Don't mock my effort!"

"Ally, that's not what Fadil is highlighting..." Edie pitches in.

Fadil looks at her in awe for speaking up in the midst of all this. He is smiling so sweetly at her, like a proud father. When I turn my head to whisper this to Daze, even he's smiling at me. He clears his throat and looks away when our eyes meet, so I am forced to face Caecilia's burning irises. She would have hit me if Daze wasn't sitting between us.

She chuckles suddenly. Somehow, even I can't take it anymore.

"You okay, Caecilia?"

Her smile looks malicious as she answers, "Hmm, yeah, I sincerely hope you all can stop pushing Daze to play along with your forced drama. Stop complicating friendships. You don't even know Ally properly to have these people link you with her!"

Her last statement directed towards Daze comes off as whiny, much to her chagrin. Though Daze's face is turned away from me, the shift in Caecilia's expression tells me it must not have been well-received.

"These days, Caecilia, it seems to me that you have a problem with everything. You keep squabbling with Ally; that day at the match, you disappeared. You didn't even inform me that you weren't coming to St. Regis on Thursday, then one or two of my mates tell me that they saw you strolling outside... Man, I don't know. It's like you're acting different around our new friend and I have no idea where this is coming from!"

A queer silence followed his monologue. Edie and I exchanged wide-eyed glances, while Fadil sat with his head in his hands.

Caecilia gasped but then quickly recovered, her voice rising in pitch, "HOW! HOW CAN YOU NOT SEE HOW SHE LOOKS

AT YOU, DAZE!? HER EYES ARE CREEPY AS SHIT! IT'S LIKE ANY MINUTE NOW, SHE MIGHT TURN INTO ONE OF THOSE KIDS FROM *VILLAGE OF THE DAMNED*!"

Ouch. It's not that bad, my eyes don't exactly light up like the headlights of a car.

"Let's not create a scene here at Dahciana's café, guys," Fadil interjects, holding his hands up cautiously at Caecilia.

Her strained voice has awakened my previously dormant headache apparently. Daze is offended at the direct attack. "What Edie pointed out, actually, is something even I'm starting to agree with. This isn't like you, Caecilia. I've known you since we were on tricycles. Just because I've branched out my friend circle, you're being truly weird!"

Running out of words, Daze turned his gaze on Fadil, who opened his mouth hesitantly. "Uhm, and yeah, what has Ally done toh you. Like, uh, it seems personal."

Caecilia runs her hands through her hair in frustration, unable to meet anyone's eyes.

"THIS," she finally spits out.

"THIS DETACHMENT that you all have suddenly developed for me, for your long time pal, for this—this, red-haired freak! Always acting smarter-than-thou and playing the innocent little lady, but I just know she is hiding something!"

"Caecilia. You need to calm down. Seriously," Eddie said, reaching across the table in an attempt to grasp her Caecilia's forearms.

Why is Edie being so supportive? Wasn't she on my side? Fadil and Daze are on mine, though. Fadil ripped the straw off his drink. "Man, I've had enough." He gulps it down.

"What do you want, Caecilia? What does it take?"

Um, wait? Is Daze giving her a free pass? What if she suggests distancing us? How is he planning to tackle whatever her choice might be? And, why wasn't I given this choice? Is.. is Daze even on my turf? Am I hallucinating?

Caecilia swings her head toward him. "What I want, Daze, is for things to go back to how they were before she appeared in our lives and tried to snatch you away just because she can! You don't even see it! Men are so dumb! She is just keeping you in her little web because she loves to exercise power. She will break your heart and your ego one day and you will come back weeping to me. But right now, you refuse to see it."

Man. This is really awkward. I can't help but feel really disengaged from this whole situation. Maybe it's some sort of self-preservation kicking in.

"So lemme get this right, madam, you're cursing him?" Daciana's voice cuts through the tension from somewhere above my head. Gosh, this headache is probably the reason I'm spacing out like this.

Exhaling loudly, Caecilia starts again with renewed vigour, "And you, miss bomb, kindly refrain from butting into our liaisons."

"We have known you for less than five days, yet here you are, spilling your unsolicited opinions all over my damn coffee. You think—"

"YOUR DAMN COFFEE is the one sponsored by Daciana here, so you better keep your nonsense between Daze and I, Caecilia." Already feeling guilty for ruining Daciana's invitation, I had to put a stop to her being dragged into our mess.

Edie, once again, takes the lead. "Daciana. We're so sorry for this, would you mind just bringing us the bill?"

Daciana clicks clacks daintily away from our table. Ashamed, I can't even look up from the burnt cloud-shaped wooden mark on our table top. When Mum and Dad used to fight behind the closed door of my room, Dad's booming voice often stated in good humour, "Darling, you know what they say. You can't live forever but you can always live in people's memories. Make your conduct impressionable. That's what I do with my eyes."

"I'm going to go pay the bill at the desk, we'll settle it later, and mind us not, we'll see you guys later too." Fadil sulkily gets up and fixes Edie with a look which makes her hurriedly shoot up as well.

At this point, I would have liked for someone to come to my rescue as well. Maybe offer me a migraine pill. Daze has other plans. "That time when we were younger and you insulted my favourite blue shirt—even then we didn't drag the quarrel for so long and with such malice. What has changed?"

"Daze," she pleaded. "That was because I apologised and saved my next month's pocket money to help you buy another! Even though it was just a mistake! It's always been me who has made adjustments in my behaviour to match yours and I've done it without any complaints just because it kept us together, I mean, on good terms. Now, for once, I am asking you to take that first step and be understanding of my place in your life!"

This conversation is getting too rom-com-y. "Uh, Caecilia, Daze has always referred to you as his best friend and I'm certain that wouldn't change. Both of you have been friends since forever and I'm not here to take the place of a buddy in Daze's life."

Take the hint sister, and keep the situation platonic.

Caecilia fixes me with a glare that could freeze hell over. I better never give anyone that type of stare with my Zaekhuru and all, otherwise someone would be detonating something for me.

"She's right!" exclaims Daze. "Both of you hold different values to me and separate places in my heart. I don't know what else there is to explain..." he trails off.

"So, I'm just a friend to you, Daze? Just a buddy? Like Fadil? Like Edie?" She seems to be on the verge of hysteria now. The group of university grads nearby are starting to give us more and more glances. A tall ginger-haired girl among them catches my eye and I offer her an apologetic smile.

Daze takes a deep breath to start again and I suddenly become aware of the mind-numbing headache I've been trying to ignore constantly. How can Caecilia act this confrontational, when just two days ago, she tried to feed me to the sharks and I'm the one holding her reputation in my palm.

"What exactly are you implying, Caecilia?!" Daze was exasperated.

"What exactly are you doing, Pippi?" Amber eyes, two inches from mine. Amber eyes, unblinking, peering into my personal dungeons.

This headache feels like there's a screw twisting inside my skull trying to break free and will succeed only when it tears it apart and shoots to freedom. It's also making me hallucinate, because his blond hair is neatly combed for once. There's a parting on one side and his rectangular ombre sunglasses are perched on top. His shirt is cream, and has some kind of brown pattern on it; maybe autumn leaves? I can't openly stare at his—well, you know, man cleavage—so bluntly when he's standing right in my face.

Wait, standing? We were sitting while having this conversation, right?

Where's uh, Caecilia? Where's Daze?

Why is everything moving in slow motion? Aaron's mouth is parted, but why aren't any words coming out?

"Pippi?"

NINE

Suddenly, there's an earthquake. Oh no. It's just me being shaken by the shoulders. But why? A girl is backing away from behind him but I can't focus my eyes on her. I think I managed to mumble out a "What?" but I am not sure.

"Do you recognise me?" His words are enunciated, and he's speaking slowly like I'm a three-year-old.

Why is he being so embarrassing? He carried me in his arms and rescued me from that dungeon, how can I ever forget FoxyJuhnson.

"FoxyJuhnson?" LOL, the word sounds funnier when he says it.

"How many fingers am I holding up?" Oh, a peace sign.

Must. Reciprocate.

Hahah. FoxyJuhnson looks tense. He definitely needs to loosen up.

WHAT. WHY DID HE HAVE TO SPLASH WATER DROPLETS ON MY FACE! MY HAIR! Now it will be all sticky and weird. Boys suck.

"Pippi. Speak to me."

His face is really close to mine. Our noses are two centimetres apart. Heat seeps from his fingers through my dress where they are wrapped around my shoulders.

"Aaron..."

"How are you feeling?" The question is followed by a palm gingerly wiping some stray moisture from my face. The gentleness makes me want to close my eyes and lean in. His hand smells faintly like new rubber tyres.

"Open your eyes."

The voice has lost its panicked edge and exudes some warmth now. Reluctantly, I open my eyes and try to look up at him.

"Do you feel like killing someone right now, Pippi?" he whispers, not vehemently, but normally, as if he's asking if I'd like some pancakes.

"No," I managed to stutter.

Speaking is an effort when my head feels so heavy. Why can't he carry me in his arms again and take me to my bed?

There is some sort of scuffle happening behind him. People are moving.

"Do you recall what happened just now?"

"Umm, Daze was, umm, talking, then…"

Why are things so hazy? Why is it so hard to recall?

"Don't try to make sense of it, just tell me what you remember." His grip around me is a little more comfortable now, but I silently pray that it's not lax.

"Okay, uhh Daze was speaking and then you switched over."

His head droops and he shakes it in disbelief. Um, let me in? "Pippi. I heard you speak to Caecilia. Do you not recall saying anything to her just now?"

"Um, no?"

"You were holding her gaze and she seemed to be in some sort of a trance and you were telling her that she wants to jump off this balcony and only that would solve her misery."

UH?

THAT CAN'T BE RIGHT! WHAT IS HE TALKING ABOUT!?

I DID NOT DO THAT!!

WHY SHOULD I BELIEVE HIM WHEN I HAVE NO MEMORY OF THIS? I WOULDN'T DO SOMETHING SO TERRIBLE!

HE IS BASICALLY IMPLYING I USED ZAEKHURU ON CAECILIA AND ENCOURAGED HER TO KILL HERSELF!

"Excuse me! I certainly did not ask her to do that! Just because I'm having some trouble concentrating because of this motherfudging severe headache, you think you can play some sick joke on me?"

"What's going on here?" Daze's voice booms and I see Caecilia trailing behind him, uncertain.

Aaron doesn't make any attempt to step back or put any distance between his body and mine. At that point, I'm almost certain that if he had, I would have lost my balance. Daze squares on Aaron.

"Oh, so this is why Caecilia came back in tears, unable to explain anything. You're going around terrorising girls now? I knew it would happen but so soon? Hah."

"Fudge off, Dexter," Juhnson plainly dismisses him. It's clear Daze's anger is bubbling up.

"Daze, wait, Aaron didn't do anything. I'm not feeling well. Listen, just answer me one thing—did I bring Caecilia here to talk or something?"

"Yeah, of course, you did. You... how do you not know this? You interrupted me, grabbed Caecilia's arm, and said you wanted to have a one-on-one. Then three minutes later, Caecilia came running, sweating like the plague and with tears in her eyes!"

Hell is caffeine-filled, man! Juhnson's story is becoming more believable by the second.

"You can let her go, dude, I'm here now." Daze's eyes are fixed pointedly at Aaron's hands which are still holding me stable.

Our eyes meet and his eyebrows are raised in concern. My assured blinking works more for his faith than my own and he gently lets me go.

"Do you want to go to the doctor?"

"Daze, I'm... I think I need some time alone, I feel like I can't breathe."

"I… don't think being alone is the best idea at this moment. I'll take you home, you can rest."

"I don't wanna go home just now, Daze. You take—you take Caecilia home."

Daze audibly deflates. "Don't keep quarrelling, guys. I can take both of you home."

How do I explain it to him that I asked that with zero sarcasm. "I'll meet you at home in an hour, okay?"

I take measured steps inside to retrieve my bag from the table. When I reach the terrace, Aaron has left. Caecilia is waiting by Daze's bike and Daze stands in contemplation.

We exchanged a glance, and I just kept walking, trying to make it clear that this was something I needed to figure out on my own. My knees were shaking and I needed somewhere to sit, but first, I had to escape my friends—a guy whom I have a crush on though I'm not sure he reciprocates my feelings, and a girl who clearly hates me as I allegedly tried to hypnotise her into jumping to her death.

If this Zaekhuru shikerdookie keeps going on like this, and I swear I will never keep any friend I make—just like these past sixteen years.

What is incomprehensible to me is how I have zero memory of asking her to do something so serious. It might be that she's making it up but this story didn't come from Daze, but from Aaron, who has nothing to do with any of us. What was he doing here anyway?

Also, I need to see a doctor about this headache as soon as I get a grip on myself. Can't deal with the possibility of using Zaekhuru to ask a doctor to end my own life next.

Caecilia and Daze zoomed by on his scooter. They make the turn on the main road, with Daze giving me one last concerned glance. Thank gosh. Now, where can I collapse?

At the exit of the premise lane, there's a tiny ice cream vendor. He must be thinking that I'm drunk, judging by how I'm leaning across his stall.

"Dexter really wanted to have his one chance to carry you to the hospital in his arms, why won't you budge?"

Juhnson was straddling his motorcycle just two feet away from me. Arms crossed across his chest; he was in no hurry now.

'Not everyone is lucky enough to have the opportunity to lift me off my feet,' is what I *feel* like saying but instead, it came out as, "Narrione lugginah to'ave d'oppORCHUH toluh..."

Well, you know what I mean.

He sighed as he dismounted and walked over to me. Very emphatically, he wrapped his hand around my right arm and gently pulled me towards his bike.

Without my permission, his hands grabbed my waist and hoisted me on the seat of his parked Apache. Once again, though I won't admit it to his face, I was thankful. Aaron stood by the handlebar. We didn't speak. My thoughts are in disarray—sedimentations and decantations occur inside my brain, and I realise I need a little bit more clarity, and the only person who can provide that is standing right here.

"Can you swear you heard me ask her to ...harm herself?"

The silence continues. There's this quote by someone about how humans are so dumb that they repeat the same actions but expect different results somehow. Unfortunately, it's wishful thinking that guides my expectations right now.

"What reason would I have to lie to you? In fact, I'm not even sure what's pulling me to hang out with you right now... not a suicide intention, I hope?" His cocked eyebrow nudged a smile onto my lips, but I swallowed it.

"You must think I'm a freak, or worse." My eyes focused on the plaster shavings falling off the brick wall in front of me.

"Nah, I don't think so," he shook his head. "I know you are."

My slight snort prompted him to continue. "Your initial plan was something else, wasn't it, when you two were having some intense conversation that day about a kidnapping in college?"

Blood chilled inside my veins. What did he just say?

WHAT ELSE HAVE I HYPNOTISED HER INTO DOING? SINCE WHEN DID I START LOSING MEMORY LIKE THIS?

Choosing my words carefully, so as not to reveal my selective memory loss, I ask, "How many times have you overheard me suggesting suspicious shxt to people?"

"Just these two times, if we don't count that day during the match when you were debating skirts versus shorts with that mousy girl you hang out with."

"When was this kidnapping incident being discussed? Was it after you found me at your place?"

"No it was… probably a day or two before that. Just bits and pieces of the conversation, but I did hear the word 'kidnapping,' and your faces were way too close, which is why, um, I kinda started paying attention because, uh, I thought you were… queer."

What I am hearing from all this nonsense is that I might have been behind my own kidnapping. Oh, gosh.

"You've been having these forgetful episodes for quite some time, right? You don't remember that conversation either, do you now?"

"These headaches, these fudging headaches must be the culprits! My focus gets a bit hazy when I get these blinding headaches."

I CAN'T BELIEVE THAT KIDNAPPING WAS A SHAM OF MY OWN INVENTION! SINCE WHEN DID THE ZAEKHURU GET SO OUT OF MY HAND!?

WHAT ELSE HAVE I DONE WITHOUT EVEN REALISING IT?

"Do you think having murderous intentions due to a headache is the telltale sign you should visit a doctor?"

I can't go to a doctor here. Our local doctor back then knew my father and hence about our ...condition. Ibuprofen will have to do it for now. No point in telling him about this.

Our reticence continued for a while before he spoke again, "Yet, why didn't that brunette brush off your directives? She was eyeing the balcony as if jumping off was her only option. You must know some huge secret of hers, and that's a talent I can applaud."

He's in a world of his own, muttering away compliments over false circumstances. HOW WILL I EXPLAIN ANYTHING TO DAZE? WHAT IF CAECILIA STARTS REMEMBERING SOME OF THE CRAP THAT I MIGHT HAVE FED INTO HER BRAIN? WHAT IF ANOTHER EPISODE LIKE THIS KIDNAPPING

AWAITS ME AND IT'S ALL MY DOING!? Also, HOW DO I MAKE THESE EPISODES STOP!?

"If you want to pull more of these scheming and plotting games, I'm your guy. I can get people to spill their guts too."

When I glanced at him, wondering what he was going on about, I saw him scratching the waistband of his jeans to show the butt of that dagger he carries around. He thinks I bullied her into acting that way. Maybe I did. Suddenly, I was extremely tired.

"What are we getting her to do next? Is her father rich? Do you want some cash?"

Not sure if he's kidding or being serious, I realise I need to explain myself. "Aaron, I want to tell you something about myself. Um, have you ever looked into someone's eyes and felt this strange, compelling force..."

*****

With thanks to:

Antara Sinha for her invaluable suggestions and silent acceptance of being the test subject

CBW for being my angel of support

Shobha Gupta for pulling this book UP

9 789369 538904

Printed by Libri Plureos GmbH in Hamburg, Germany